If your heart beats passionately for people who have wandered far from God, you need to read this book today! In *Eats with Sinners*, Arron Chambers reminds us of the power of love in reaching people for Jesus. He reminds us that love is always the best context through which to share the truth. And he reminds us that there are no lost causes.

MARK BATTERSON
New York Times bestselling author of *The Circle Maker* and lead pastor of National Community Church

I love that each chapter of this book focuses on a character trait that Christians should cultivate. God always wants to do work *in* us before he works *through* us. Let this book help mold your heart as the Spirit changes you—and then he may just use you to change the lives of the people around you.

KYLE IDLEMAN
Bestselling author of *Not a Fan* and *Grace Is Greater*

It's so easy to forget that the people who live on our streets, who we see on the news, who believe differently than we do, whose lifestyles may make us uncomfortable, all bear the holy image of God and carry the same fears, the same loneliness, the same ultimate longings that Christians do. *Eats with Sinners* is a gentle call to emulate a God who, when we were still far off, met us in Christ and brought us home.

ANDREW PETERSON
Singer/songwriter

Arron Chambers's passion and heart for people come through powerfully in *Eats with Sinners*. This is a fantastic resource for all of us to be reminded and challenged by the way of Jesus. Arron points to how we can engage people with the purpose of Jesus in practical and inspiring ways.

JUD WILHITE
Senior pastor of Central Church

Jesus was called a friend of sinners. We are supposed to be friends with sinners. In fact, if you're not close to people who are far from God, you may not be as close to God as you think you are, because God's heart is always with those who are far from him. In *Eats with Sinners*, Arron Chambers will inspire you to get closer to some people who are far from God and love them as Jesus did.

VINCE ANTONUCCI
Lead pastor of Verve Church and author of *God for the Rest of Us*

Thanks for your book. Thanks for your heart. My wife mentioned the other day on the way home from church, "How can *one* book make such an impact on our whole church?"

ALLEN GONZALEZ
Preaching minister at Capital City Christian Church

Our series on *Eats with Sinners* is going great. People are being baptized, joining the church, and reaching the lost. Exciting times! I cannot truly express the impact Arron's book is having on our church. It is changing hearts and changing lives.

JOHN FAULKNER
Director at Northside Christian Academy

EATS WITH SINNERS

Loving Like Jesus

ARRON CHAMBERS

NAVPRESS

*A NavPress resource published in alliance
with Tyndale House Publishers, Inc.*

NAVPRESS⬤®

NavPress is the publishing ministry of The Navigators, an international Christian organization and leader in personal spiritual development. NavPress is committed to helping people grow spiritually and enjoy lives of meaning and hope through personal and group resources that are biblically rooted, culturally relevant, and highly practical.

For more information, visit www.NavPress.com.

The Team:
Don Pape, Publisher
David Zimmerman, Editor
Dean H. Renninger, Designer

Cover illustrations by Free Design File. All rights reserved.

Author photo by Stephany Jenkins, copyright © 2015. All rights reserved.

Published in association with The Blythe Daniel Agency, Inc., P.O. Box 64197, Colorado Springs, CO 80962.

For information about special discounts for bulk purchases, please contact Tyndale House Publishers at csresponse@tyndale.com, or call 1-800-323-9400.

Cataloging-in-Publication Data is available.

ISBN 978-1-63146-832-2

Printed in the United States of America

23	22	21	20	19	18	17
7	6	5	4	3	2	1

*To Journey Christian Church—a body of
devotees who are friendly with sinners.
Thanks for eating with this sinner every week and for doing
your part to make sure the banquet hall in heaven is full.*

Contents

Foreword

I remember when I first met Arron Chambers. At the time, I was leading a church that was growing at a fast pace. The increasing attendance, however, didn't compare to the increasing frustration that kept me up at night.

The influx of people was from other churches; very few identified as non-Christian. In my sermons, personal conversations, newsletters, social media updates, and in other ways, I tried to cast a vision of engaging people far from God with the love of God. While some church members grabbed hold of the vision, far more seemed comfortable with not sharing the message of Jesus.

When my disappointment was at its highest, I decided to attend a leadership conference for some encouragement. Between the conference's main sessions, I became acquainted with Arron. After the last session of the day, we grabbed dinner. That evening, in a small restaurant at an Irvine, Texas, hotel, I poured out my heart. While my monologue may have seemed unending to most people, Arron sat patiently across the table and listened. After I was done venting, he conveyed some of the foundational points of this book. Inspired by his insight, wisdom, and passion for all people, I returned to my church with renewed excitement! Even today, I regularly leverage the principles Arron shared to help others love the people Jesus loved. I've had many meals with people, but that dinner is one I won't soon forget.

Before you begin this journey with Arron, let me prepare you a little. If you consider yourself a Christian, then approach this book with an open mind, a compassionate heart, and a willingness to change your life. Why? Because Arron isn't content with any Christian "doing life as usual" if that involves indifference toward those far from God. He won't allow us to hide behind powerful words or lengthy prayers for people when we do nothing to reach them. And I'm sure you care too much about your loved ones to keep the gospel a secret.

I believe it's almost impossible to read this book and not develop an excitement to introduce people to God.

For those who might not be following Jesus, let me encourage you. It could be that when you first saw the title of this book, you took offense at the word *sinners*. Maybe you've been called a sinner because you don't follow Jesus, or maybe someone you know has been called that. The word *sinner* just sounds bad. I mean, who wouldn't take offense at it? I do!

But that's the point—we're all undeserving sinners in need of God's love. As you turn the pages of this book, you'll be introduced to Jesus in a way that might surprise you. You'll see a Jesus who will eat with anyone, doesn't run from controversy, is anything but traditional, values the marginalized, speaks truth in love, and is willing to do whatever it takes to have a relationship with you!

Thank you, Arron. I'm grateful for that dinner so many years ago where you reminded me that Jesus would indeed share a meal with anyone—even sinners like you and me.

Caleb Kaltenbach
Lead pastor of Discovery Church and author of
Messy Grace and *God of Tomorrow*

A Word Before

Before I start this book, and before you start reading, I need to say two things.

First, I love sinners. We're all sinners. If you are a Christian, you're a sinner saved by grace. That should make you humble as you eat with sinners and share the grace of Jesus. The best appetizer before eating with sinners is a slice of humble pie.

If you are not a Christian, I want you to know that Jesus loves you more than his life itself. The fourth book of the New Testament records that Jesus said, "God so loved the world that he gave his one and only Son, that whoever believes in him shall not perish but have eternal life. For God did not send his Son into the world to condemn the world, but to save the world through him" (John 3:16-17). God sent his Son, Jesus, to this world to die on a cross for your sins because he loves you and wants you to spend eternity with him in heaven. I love you too, and I would love to eat with you sometime—if another Christ follower doesn't beat me to it.

Second, I love the church. If you are my brother or sister in Christ, I want you to know right now that I love you, because there may be points in this book where you start to wonder whether I really like the church.

I say some strong things about the church and address issues that may not reflect your experience. If that's the case, I praise God that you're part of one that gets it. Just know that there are also some well-intentioned believers who don't get it and need a not-so-subtle reminder that our work is not done.

Here's the bottom line:

I love Jesus.

I love you.

Jesus loves lost people.

He wants us to love lost people, too.

Every word of this book was written with love and a hunger for more Christians to eat with sinners.

A friend of mine was visiting his mentor, a retired preacher, in the hospital; his mentor was preparing to say farewell to his wife of more than fifty years. As my friend wrestled with finding the right words to bring peace to his mentor in his time of need, his mentor reached out, patted his knee, and said, "It's okay. I haven't been preaching fairy tales all these years."

I'm not preaching fairy tales in this book. I believe what I've written, but—more importantly—I'm living it.

I was called to serve at Journey Christian Church in Greeley, Colorado, in the summer of 2008, shortly before the first edition of this book was released. Upon arriving at

Journey, a church of about three hundred at the time, I began to immediately implement the lessons of this book. By the end of 2009 our average attendance had grown to more than four hundred.

In 2010, I took the church through the thirteen lessons in this book and then another six-week study we called "The Party."[1] If I hadn't experienced the results of that Eats with Sinners study myself, it would be hard to believe. It would seem like a fairy tale.

During the nineteen weeks of our first Eats with Sinners church-wide study in 2010,[2] our average attendance grew by more than 150. As people started introducing their friends, family, and neighbors to Jesus through intentional relationships, we also started to see people give their lives to Christ in droves. After the sermon on week sixteen of that first Eats with Sinners study, I presented the gospel, many people responded, and we baptized 52 people that day. We ended up baptizing 102 people before the end of 2010, and we've baptized 632 people in the last six years. Our average weekly attendance has grown to more than 1,000 as of this writing.

Now, I know that it's not all about numbers, but it *is* all about loving Jesus and loving like him. We celebrate each lost person who finds Jesus through a loving relationship and is now counted among the saved because someone loved them enough to eat with them.

Introduction

Some of My Best Friends Are Lost

To some, *Lost* is a highly addictive TV show from the mid-2000s about the survivors of a plane wreck who found themselves on a deserted island where nothing made sense and they were not alone.

Lost might be a zone where single socks, class rings, your favorite hat, sunglasses, my brother's car keys, glass eyeballs,[1] the Watergate tapes, and my six-toed cat (Sasquatch) dwell while waiting to be found . . . or not.

Lost is how Ming Kuang Chen felt in an elevator in the Bronx. Chen was making a delivery to a high-rise apartment when the elevator he was riding malfunctioned and dropped almost thirty floors, stranding Chen between the third and fourth floors. Chen screamed, pressed the alarm button, and banged on the elevator door— but for three days no one heard his cries for help and no one looked for him.[2]

Being lost is never fun. Being lost and realizing that no one is looking for you is even worse.

Being lost is never fun. Being lost and realizing that no one is looking for you is even worse.

To God, *lost* describes people who are not where they are supposed to be; *found* describes people who are exactly where they are supposed to be—with him, in Jesus. "There is now no condemnation for those who are *in Christ Jesus*" (Romans 8:1, emphasis added). God prefers that people be found rather than lost, so he sent his Son into this world to find and save them.

Jesus was a magnet for lost people. They were drawn to him because he was drawn to them. The rejected found acceptance, the hurt found healing, the judged found the Judge to be surprisingly nonjudgmental. The Gospel writer Luke penned these words: "The tax collectors and sinners were all gathering around to hear Jesus. But the Pharisees and the teachers of the law muttered, 'This man welcomes sinners and eats with them'" (Luke 15:1-2). The Pharisees were the religious leaders of Jesus' day. *Sinners* was a term the Pharisees and teachers of God's law used to identify lawbreakers—people they considered social pariahs and so morally filthy they had to be avoided at all costs. *Sinners* was a term the Pharisees used to justify marginalizing people whose behavior they found reprehensible, to identify people they viewed as beyond the hopes of salvation. I've found it's almost impossible to love someone you've labeled. That being said, *sinners* was a term the Pharisees used to label people they didn't want to have to love or feel guilty for not loving.

There are not degrees of true love.

Jesus truly loved sinners, so he ate with them.

Jesus ate with people the Pharisees crossed the road to avoid.

Jesus ate with people we cross the street to avoid.

Why? He truly loved people, even though he didn't like their sin.

There are not degrees of sin.

We're all sinners (Romans 3:23).

Sinners was a term Jesus used to identify people who have missed the mark, and we've all missed the mark—in the past, now, and every second of our lives this side of heaven. Yet Jesus still eats with us here on earth because he wants to eat with us for all eternity.

So, ironically, the Pharisees were right about Jesus: He *was* welcoming sinners and eating with them. He was eating with sinners even when he was eating with Pharisees. You eat with a sinner every time you eat with me, and I eat with a sinner every time I eat with you. The Pharisees missed the mark by missing the point that we're all in need of salvation. We miss the mark when we forget the same thing.

Let me pause here and make an important point: As I mentioned earlier, the methods in this book work. I've used them over the years to reach many people for Christ. Eating with sinners, or building intentional relationships with lost people through which they can be introduced to Jesus, is the most effective way I know to reach people for Christ. But I also want you to know that I have to be very intentional about interacting with lost people, because for many years, as a preacher at a Christian church, I became insulated and isolated from lost people.

It wasn't always like that. I used to be immersed in a world of lost people. I rode my Big Wheel with them. I sat next to them in school. In the cafeteria, I traded my last piece of Bazooka bubble gum for their chocolate milk. We played soccer together, went to see *Footloose* together, skated all-skates together at Sun State skating rink, danced to "Rock Lobster" together, laughed together, took driver's ed together, went to Just Say No to Drugs assemblies together, took the SAT together, graduated together, and waited tables together. But eventually my encounters with lost people became fewer and further apart.

Today, because of the lessons I learned from Jesus in the Gospel of Luke, I am very intentional about building relationships with lost people. Because of what I've learned about the power and importance of eating with sinners, I am in a very different place and very different places.

I sold my weight set and joined a local gym instead of adding to my home gym.

I seek out opportunities to get involved with the local government to work on community projects. My family and I partnered with our community to build a $1.3 million universally accessible playground called Aven's Village.[3]

For the past few years, on my days off and most evenings throughout the year, I coach track, cross-country, and basketball at a local public high school, Frontier Academy. Coaching allows me to build relationships with a lot of great people in our community.

It's through coaching that I met a young man named Joel. Joel's father has never been in the picture but showed up just before his graduation with an armful of gifts. After practice one day Joel was talking with me about his dad and said through tears, "I don't want his stuff! I just want him not to leave!"

I've been praying for Joel, an avowed atheist, for more than two years and spent countless hours with him at practice and meets. I love this young man. His dad disappeared again after Joel's graduation, so my wife and I invited him to spend Father's Day with us. He came to church that day and ate lunch with us. It was great to worship with Joel, eat with him, and get to know him even better.

I didn't see or hear from Joel again until a few weeks ago. I was working late at the church when someone told me that a young man was asking to see me. I'm typically not there that late, but I now know that God had arranged a divine appointment. Joel was looking for me and just wanted to talk, so I invited him to my office and we spent a couple of hours together. He's lost, confused, hurting, and broken. He trusts me because I've coached him almost every day for more than two years. He knows I love him, so when he asked me to explain how he could have the hope I have, I had the chance to present the gospel to him and introduce him to Jesus.

I wouldn't trade that conversation with Joel for anything.

I am very passionate about building intentional relationships with lost people so I can introduce them to Jesus Christ, so I'm very intentional with my time. I'm intentional about spending time with other Christians (Hebrews 10:25), but I'm also intentional about spending time being salt and light around lost people in my world (Matthew 5:13-15).

JESUS ATE WITH LOST PEOPLE

As religious leaders, the Pharisees were committed to the law—and that should have been reflected in a deeper commitment to God and his people. But it wasn't. Instead, their commitment to God resulted in neglect of the weak, poor, and needy.

Once, a Pharisee invited Jesus home for a meal, so Jesus went to the Pharisee's house and ate with him. The Pharisee noticed that Jesus didn't wash his hands before the meal. This surprised him, and he asked Jesus about it. Jesus—struck by the irony of the situation—seized an opportunity to teach this man and his guests an impor-

The heart is the heart of the matter. God designed our hearts to beat for others.

tant lesson on the true application of God's law (Luke 11:37-54).

Jesus pointed out that although someone eating with dirty hands upset the Pharisees—and this one in particular—they seemed indifferent about serving God with a dirty heart. They cleaned the outside of the cup but neglected the greed and wickedness filling the inside. Referring to the Pharisees' hearts, Jesus said, "You foolish people! Did not the one who made the outside make the inside also? But . . . be generous to the poor, and everything will be clean for you" (Luke 11:40-41).

The heart is the heart of the matter. God designed our hearts to beat for other people: lost *and* found, easy to love *and* hard to love, rich *and* poor, and those with clean hands *and* those with dirty hands. Jesus was teaching this Pharisee that God made our insides to love *all* people—including "outsiders." Jesus lambasted the Pharisees and the experts in the law for giving their hearts to their perverted interpretation of the law of God but not to the maker of the law and the people for whom the law was written. True commitment to God does not result in legalism, but love; not harm, but help; not pride, but humility; not judgment, but mercy; not isolation, but interaction; not rules over people, but relationships with people. True commitment to God results in lost people being found, because true commitment to God results in lost people being loved.

Jesus eagerly ate with sinners on earth because he longed to eat with them in heaven. Jesus referred to himself as the bridegroom (Luke 5:34-35) putting on a great banquet meal (Luke 14:13-24) that he will one day eat in the Kingdom of Heaven with everyone who accepts his invitation. Jesus' love for lost people was so great, he was willing not just to eat with sinners but also to die for them on a cross: "Greater love has no one than this: to lay down one's life for one's friends" (John 15:13). The Pharisees obsessed about ritualistic sacrifices for God, but because of the cross, Christians should be obsessed with loving sacrifices for others, doing whatever it takes to reach lost people with the hopeful message of Jesus.

Doing whatever it takes means that we may need to put to rest the methods we've used in the past to communicate with lost people. Some of our presentations of the gospel—from pulpits, from the pages of our literature, and from our attempts to share our faith directly—have included an overabundance of yelling, pulpit pounding, finger shaking, foot stomping, and pronouncements that unless people accept a "loving" Jesus, he will send them to spend eternity in a burning lake of fire where worms don't die and the wicked weep and gnash their teeth forever.

That's not the Jesus I see on the pages of my Bible.

I see grace.

I see truth.

I see love.

I see a loving Messiah dispensing hope to lost people, one meal at a time.

EVANGELISM = RELATIONSHIPS

Eating with sinners is not really about eating. Well, it is, but it's really about relationships. Jesus ate food with people because he wanted to build relationships with them. That's what has happened at every table around which you've spent any amount of time. Every table, given enough time, comes to life, reaches out, and connects those gathered around it with the roots of relationships. This is why I want to eat less often with saints and more often with sinners. I want some of my best friends to be lost—but not for long.

In some of Jesus' last words to his disciples, he said, "The Messiah will suffer and rise from the dead on the third day, and repentance for the forgiveness of sins will be preached in his name to all nations, beginning at Jerusalem" (Luke 24:46-47).

You can't miss the point. There are lost people in "all nations," and Jesus expects all Christians to go to where those people are wandering, find them, and eat with them.

I'll discuss this in more detail later, but it's important to point out that eating with someone in the ancient world was much more significant than most of us modern people will ever understand. To eat with someone was a statement of hospitality, acceptance, tolerance, and intimacy. Living with this understanding of mealtime made people in the ancient world much more aware of with whom they chose to eat.

It was one thing for Jesus to welcome sinners, but it was something else altogether for Jesus to eat with them. Jesus shared a table with sinners because he wanted to have a relationship with them.

I want some of my best friends to be lost—but not for long.

Relationships are the key to reaching lost people. I define evangelism as "an intentional relationship through which someone is introduced to Jesus Christ." Healthy relationships are essential if we want to have the kind of life God intended for all of us, and they are also essential if we want to reach lost people as Jesus did.

In *Growing God's Church: How People Are Actually Coming to Faith Today,* an interesting study of how lost people come to faith, Dr. Gary McIntosh reveals the results of a survey of nearly a thousand Christians over a period of ten years. One of the questions he asked was, "How did you come to faith?" His results reveal the power of relationships in reaching lost people with the gospel. According to his research, most people (43.2 percent) come to Christ through a relationship with a family member. Other responses included relationships with a church staff member (17.3 percent), a friend (15.7 percent), a lay teacher (8.3 percent), a neighbor (2.9 percent), and last by a work colleague (1.8 percent). So according to McIntosh's research, approximately 73.5 percent of those surveyed pointed to a relationship with another Christian as the context through which they were introduced to Jesus. A few years ago the Institute for American Church Growth (today known as Church Growth, Inc.) asked more than ten thousand people, "What or who was responsible for your coming to Christ and your church?"

More than 75 percent responded that a friend or relative had invited them.[4]

The survey proves what you might already suspect: Most people come to a saving faith in Jesus through an intentional relationship. An intentional relationship for a Christian is one in which one person intends to one day have the chance to introduce the other person to Jesus—and then one day *does* introduce him or her to Jesus. And there is no more scriptural model for building relationships with lost people than eating with them.

The word *church* means "called-out ones." Christians are called to be different from all the hazardous influences in the world. Perhaps we have taken that too far, with too many of us deserting the very world Jesus expects us to impact. We are faithful in meeting with other saints regularly around the Lord's Table, but are we faithless in our refusal to meet with lost people around theirs?

This can change. It must change: one relationship at a time, one meal at a time.

In this book, as we examine Jesus' evangelistic strategy in the Gospel of Luke, we'll see all the ingredients that went into his perfect recipe for reaching lost people. My hope is that, as you embark

An intentional relationship for a Christian is one in which one person intends to one day have the chance to introduce the other person to Jesus— and then one day does introduce him or her to Jesus.

on practicing the principles that follow, you'll discover the power of eating with sinners and the joy of knowing that some of your best friends have been found.

1
INTEGRITY

Jesus, full of the Holy Spirit, left the Jordan and was led
by the Spirit into the wilderness, where for forty days
he was tempted by the devil.

LUKE 4:1-2

I want you to understand that lacking integrity is our problem, not God's. Like true north, God is a fixed point of reference that never changes and will always be exactly where he's supposed to be.

People, on the other hand, aren't always trustworthy. We're all over the place, so we have to sign contracts, put our right hand on the Bible, pay deposits, and back up our word by saying, "Cross my heart, hope to die, stick a needle in my eye." (Stick a needle in my eye? Who comes up with this stuff . . . the CIA?)

My friend Gary Mello from Orlando told me a story from his high school days. He worked on a 125-foot scallop

1

boat, the *Rodman Swift IV*, that sailed out of New Bedford, Massachusetts. Hard and dangerous work, scalloping paid well, and many young men jumped at the chance to fish for scallops in the North Atlantic. The crew worked long hours, rotating shifts and manning every station during all hours of the day and night.

Like true north, God is a fixed point of reference that never changes and will always be exactly where he's supposed to be.

One evening they put out from New Bedford on an eight-hour trip that would take them past Nantucket to the scalloping grounds in the Atlantic. Early in the trip Gary was assigned to the wheelhouse and told not to touch anything but to watch the steering compass and make sure the boat stayed on course. The gyro repeater (a steering compass) had been set to a heading of 280 degrees N, so the ship was set to autopilot to its destination. A gyro repeater steers the ship to the coordinates determined and set by the captain. It's a complicated system that works extremely well because of the dependability of the magnetic pull of true north. Gary was simply to make sure that the ship didn't deviate off course.

"No problem," Gary replied, as he took his seat next to the compass and prepared for a long and boring night.

At some point, early in the evening, Gary became thirsty. Knowing he couldn't leave his post, he hollered to his friend Stoney to bring him a canned soft drink. Gary finished his Coke, set it next to the compass, and returned to intermittent glances at the compass and the nautical maps he had secured to figure out where the boat was heading.

Hours passed, and Gary started to grow concerned because he was sure that he was starting to see land out of the window on the starboard side. The compass still pointed at 280 degrees N, which would be taking them away from land and far out to sea for an early-morning rendezvous with the fishing ground, so he figured he was mistaken and tried to relax. But something didn't feel right.

Eventually his concern grew to the point that he felt compelled to leave his post and tell the captain. Into the damp darkness of the captain's quarters, connected to the wheelhouse, Gary softly whispered, "Cap, I'm not sure we're heading in the right direction."

Half asleep, the captain asked if the compass still pointed to 280 degrees N.

"Yes," Gary replied.

"Then I'm sure we're fine. You're probably just seeing ground fog. Don't worry about it."

With the captain's reassurance, Gary made his way back to his post, convinced that if the captain wasn't worried, then he shouldn't be either.

Several hours passed as the ship steamed toward its early-morning appointment with a multitude of mid-Atlantic scal-

Integrity is doing the right thing, even if nobody is watching.

—UNKNOWN

lops. Everything seemed okay until the first light of morning confirmed Gary's worst nightmare. Land!

In a panic, he interrupted the captain's slumber one more time. "Captain," Gary whispered, "I think I'm seeing land."

"It's just ground fog," the captain muttered.

3

Convinced that something was amiss, Gary shouted, "No, I'm seeing land!"

"Impossible!" the captain grumbled as he quickly dressed and headed to the wheelhouse, where he verified Gary's fears. The ship was not heading 280 degrees N, but south down the coast to Long Island, New York!

"Gary, what did you do?"

"Nothing. I just sat here and stared at that compass all night long like you told me to."

"Did this compass stay on 280 degrees N all night?"

"Yes, sir. And I haven't left the wheelhouse except to get you."

The captain reset the compass while he searched for some reason for the deviation. It didn't take too long to identify the source of the problem. "Gary, is this your can of soda?"

It was.

"The metal in your soda can messed with the magnet in the compass, and it's caused the whole ship to deviate off course! Do you see what you did?" the captain shouted.

The can had disrupted the magnetic field around the compass, and the *Rodman Swift IV* and her crew went eight hours off course. Gary learned an important lesson about compasses, magnets, navigation, and the ability of a scallop-boat captain to invent new curse words when he is extremely angry. He also learned how easily a ship can be pulled off course by something as simple as a soft-drink can.

If we want to be effective in reaching lost people, we must be people of integrity—fixed points of reference that people can follow to find their way to God. One impurity in our lives can easily pull us—and the lost people who know us—off course.

Jesus had integrity. Like true north, his life was a fixed point of reference that others could follow to find their way to God.

Understanding the importance of pointing people to God—and his role as the way—Jesus, with hair still damp with the waters of baptism and with the loving words of an approving Father ringing in his ears, followed the Holy Spirit into the desert. For forty days he was tempted by the devil. His mission to find wayward people began with allowing himself to be led away—into the desert—and having his integrity confirmed through testing, testing that was essential to the success of his ministry and the key to his understanding our struggles.

If Jesus had fallen in the desert, there would have been no hope for this fallen world, so it's a good thing that he did the good thing when tempted. In the desert and throughout his life, Jesus was "tempted in

Oh! Almighty and Everlasting God, Creator of Heaven, Earth and the Universe: Help me to be, to think, to act what is right, because it is right; make me truthful, honest and honorable in all things; make me intellectually honest for the sake of right and honor and without thought of reward to me. Give me the ability to be charitable, forgiving and patient with my fellowmen—help me to understand their motives and their shortcomings—even as Thou understandest mine! Amen, Amen, Amen.

—PRESIDENT HARRY TRUMAN'S PRAYER FOR INTEGRITY

every way, just as we are" (Hebrews 4:15), but he did not sin—an example of both the reality and power of integrity.

I believe that before we can truly help lost people find their way through the desert of temptation and back to the Father, we must, like Jesus, survive our own deserts of temptation—defining moments when we grow into more or shrink into less. Jesus' ministry to reach lost people began with a defining moment in the wilderness when he had to choose (three times, actually) between right and wrong. Would he give in to temptation, become just another sinner, and hinder his ministry? Or would he do the right thing? He chose to do the right thing.

If Jesus had fallen in the desert, there would have been no hope for this fallen world, so it's a good thing that he did the good thing when tempted.

Unlike Jesus, we are not perfect. We all sin. But that doesn't mean we can't be people of integrity. In the end, for people who aren't going to die on a cross for the sins of the world, a life of integrity is not defined by a moment of weakness. We are going to make mistakes, but that doesn't mean that we can't be used by God to make a difference, if we'll only learn from our mistakes and refuse to let them pull our lives off course and away from integrity.

Living a life of integrity is essential if we want to have a truly effective ministry. You can have integrity without a ministry, but you can't have a ministry without integrity.

This is why God required the high priest, under the old covenant, on the Day of Atonement, to clean himself before entering God's presence. The high priest was to bathe before putting on the sacred garments (Leviticus 16:4) and to deal with his own sins before dealing with the sins of the people. Before he shed one drop of animal blood to atone for someone else's sin, the high priest had to shed the blood of a bull for his own sin and the sin of his household (Leviticus 16:6, 11).

I think God required that the high priest make his first act of ministry to himself and his household because our personal and private holiness should be our priority. If we aren't walking with integrity privately before God, we can't truly walk with integrity publicly for God. God values a good heart more than a good performance. God values sincere private integrity more than a hypocritical public ministry. God is the definition of integrity, and the priest was God's representative to the people, so it was essential for him to be godly and to have integrity—not faultless, but false-less.

This is why God wants us, his priests (1 Peter 2:5, 9; Revelation 1:6; 5:10), to be people of integrity before we begin our ministry to lost people.

It's the purpose behind the whole log-in-the-eye story that Jesus told in his most well-known sermon. Trying to teach us the importance of dealing with our own integrity issues before attempting to help others with theirs, Jesus said,

> Why do you look at the speck of sawdust in your brother's eye and pay no attention to the plank in your own eye? . . . You hypocrite, first take the plank out of your eye, and then you will see clearly to remove the speck from your brother's eye.
>
> LUKE 6:41-42

What a hilarious picture! What important truths for each of us to remember before we eat the first morsel of food with a lost person!

First, Jesus *does* want us to get specks out of other people's eyes. Don't miss that point.

Second—which really comes first—before we attempt to get *specks* out of other people's eyes, we must first take the *planks* out of our own eyes. Pretty humbling. But Jesus wants our ministries to be characterized by integrity, not hypocrisy. Hypocrisy is cancerous to evangelism, rendering Jesus a joke and his message a punch line in the hearts and minds of lost people.

PERSONAL INTEGRITY PRODUCES AUTHENTICITY, NOT HYPOCRISY

I believe it all begins with personal integrity. Our integrity is the foundation upon which God can build a significant life and ministry. Without personal integrity, our lives will ultimately come crashing down. Without personal integrity, our public ministry is inauthentic and ultimately hypocritical. Let me say it another way: Authenticity is what integrity wears when it goes out in public. A familiar story may help you to see what I'm saying here.

One of my favorite Hans Christian Andersen fables describes an emperor who is arguably the most famous hypocrite of all time. The emperor loved new clothes. One day two swindlers came to his city and made people believe they were weavers who could manufacture the finest cloth imaginable—but the quality of the cloth was so high, the clothes would be invisible to anyone who was not very discerning or was unpardonably stupid. These charlatans worked hard but made nothing.

When the emperor was shown his "new outfit," he acted impressed even though he saw nothing, and he agreed to wear the outfit in a parade through his kingdom. As he marched through the streets, everyone who saw him cried out, "Indeed, the emperor's new suit is incomparable! What a wonderful suit!" The people didn't want others to know they saw nothing. The universal praise continued until the emperor passed by a little child who cried out, "The emperor's not wearing any clothes!"

At this, everyone in the kingdom acknowledged the same fact and joined the child in proclaiming, "The emperor's not wearing any clothes!" The charade was over.

Our charade must end too.

Just as sure as that delusional emperor was buck naked and needed to admit it, you and I are sinners who need to get authentic and admit both our tendency to sin and our need of salvation. We're all sinners who fall short of the glory of God (Romans 3:23). Let's be authentic and admit it.

PERSONAL INTEGRITY PRODUCES COURAGE, NOT FEAR

Integrity doesn't just manifest itself in authenticity; it also manifests itself in courage.

Telemachus was a man of integrity who faced his fears and

in so doing saved lives and pointed lost people to God. The story is told of how Telemachus followed the crowds to the Colosseum in Rome and watched sadly as two gladiators fought to the death. Telemachus tried to get between them, shouting, "In the name of Christ, stop!" Enraged that this man was interrupting their entertainment, the crowd stoned Telemachus. When the people came to their senses and saw the monk lying dead in a pool of blood, they fell silent and left the stadium. According to tradition, because of Telemachus's death, three days later the emperor ended the practice of gladiators fighting to the death.[1]

You and I are sinners who need to get authentic and admit both our tendency to sin and our need of salvation.

"The wicked flee though no one pursues, but the righteous are as bold as a lion" (Proverbs 28:1). Telemachus was as bold as a lion, and we should be too.

To reach this world with the saving message of Jesus Christ, we're going to have to be courageous—and we will be, if we are also righteous.

Sin makes cowards of us all.

A father who smoked pot in college may be afraid to tell his son to say no to drugs.

A mother who slept with other men before marriage may feel intimidated about trying to persuade her eighteen-year-old daughter to save herself for marriage.

The pastor who struggles with an addiction to pornography may find it impossible to preach against the very monster that privately stalks him late at night while his family sleeps upstairs.

Discovery of Truth

I met Jeff when I moved to Florida. We both worked at Home Depot and enjoyed surfing. One Saturday I asked Jeff if he wanted to go surfing the next day. He mentioned that he was going to church. I didn't know at the time that he was a Bible college student and a committed Christian. I was interested in going to church, since I was a thousand miles from home and lonely.

I didn't go to church with Jeff the next day, but a seed was planted. Over the next few months, Jeff and I had many talks about life. He was a frank and to-the-point kind of guy. He never seemed to hesitate to say what I needed to hear to challenge my way of thinking.

Jeff was a man of integrity, and I grew to respect him. Jeff led me to Christ and helped me get plugged in with the church, and I eventually went to Bible college, where I continued to grow in my faith. And to think it all started when I asked a coworker to go surfing.

—SHAWN—

Private sin is an evil warden that Satan employs to keep us locked up, silent, and hopeless in a dungeon that reeks with fear. But private sin is also an illusion. We can't fool God.

God searches our hearts (1 Chronicles 28:9; Psalm 7:9; Romans 8:27; Revelation 2:23) and knows the sins we struggle with. He stands ready to "forgive us our sins and purify us from all unrighteousness" (1 John 1:9). His forgiveness, and his forgiveness alone, makes us righteous—people with integrity who should be courageous in the face of sin and sinners.

PERSONAL INTEGRITY PRODUCES FAITHFULNESS, NOT PERFECTION

Men and women with integrity are unstoppable. You can be unstoppable. When Nehemiah needed someone to make sure the gates in the newly rebuilt walls around Jerusalem were not opened until the right time, he called on a man named Hananiah, "because he was a man of integrity and feared God more than most people do" (Nehemiah 7:2).

When Satan wanted a man to prove human frailty, God offered him a man of integrity who would be faithful to the end, saying, "Have you considered my servant Job? There is no one on earth like him; he is blameless and upright, a man who fears God and shuns evil" (Job 2:3).

These men were faithful—not perfect.

Think about King David, the man who slept with a woman who was not his wife (Bathsheba) and then had her husband killed in battle. The apostle Paul reminds us of what God thought about David: "I have found David son of Jesse, a man after my own heart" (Acts 13:22). God said this not because David was perfect, but because David was faithful (Hebrews 11:32-33). Yes, David was a sinner, but he didn't allow himself to be defined by sin. He was a man who, when confronted about his sin by the prophet Nathan, admitted he was a sinner (2 Samuel 12:13) and took significant steps to mend his character. David's life was not defined by a moment of weakness.

God told Solomon, David's son, to follow his dad's example: "If you walk before me faithfully with integrity of heart and uprightness, as David your father did, . . . I will establish your royal throne over Israel forever" (1 Kings 9:4-5). God wanted Solomon to look at his father's life as a point of reference—not because David was perfect, but because he was faithful. And David was faithful because he had integrity. God wants us to be people of integrity.

When Satan wanted a man to prove human frailty, God offered him a man of integrity who would be faithful to the end.

Why does God call us to be people of integrity? First, for our own good. And second, he doesn't want our lives to pull off course the lives of the lost people who are following us.

Delmar, who used to be an elder at Journey Christian Church before his death, was a man of integrity. Delmar led a Saturday morning Bible study at a local bar called The Fort (which I'll discuss more in chapter 5). Since Delmar walked with integrity, he was able to walk into the world and lives of all kinds of people. His integrity gave him the opportunity to reach people with the gospel in a place where they feel comfortable.

He reached a lot of people for Jesus because his life was a fixed point that the people at The Fort could follow straight to Jesus.

Those people at The Fort didn't realize it, but they needed Delmar to be a man of integrity. They need us to be people of integrity: fixed points of reference they can follow to find themselves not lost—not heading south to Long Island, not even heading 280 degrees N—but heading back to where they were supposed to be all the time.

WALKING WITH INTEGRITY

- Invest in personal devotions. Get your Bible, find a quiet place, and start reading the book of Luke. After reading for a while, stop and spend some time in prayer. Ask God to help you identify the areas in your life that are not as pure as they should be.

- Find an accountability partner. I meet with other Christians every week for the sole purpose of ensuring that I'm growing in my faith and living the kind of life I should be living. Find a Christian of the same gender with whom you can meet regularly and by whom you can be held accountable for living a life of integrity.

- Get involved with a local church. Are you regularly meeting with a local church? If not, it's time to get involved with one. This will put you in fellowship with other Christians and in a place where you will be exposed to biblical teaching—both of which will help you to live a life of integrity.

2
ACCESSIBILITY

Jesus returned to Galilee . . . He was teaching in their
synagogues, and everyone praised him.

LUKE 4:14-15

A man working on a construction site accidentally shot a nail into his left hand with his nail gun. The construction site happened to be across the street from a hospital, so the man walked off the site, across the street, and into the hospital to receive medical attention.

Upon entering the foyer, he found a simple room—one table, a chair, a plant in the corner, and two doors: one marked "Emergency" and the other "Non-Emergency." He looked at his hand and thought, *It's not that bad,* so he chose the door marked "Non-Emergency."

As he passed through the door, he found himself in another simple room—one table, a chair, a plant in the corner, and two doors: "Internal" and "External." Aware that his injury was obviously external, he chose the door marked "External."

As he passed through the door, he found himself in a simple room—one table, a chair, a plant in the corner, and two doors: "Severe Pain" and "Mild Pain." Not hurting too much, he chose the door marked "Mild Pain."

As he passed through the door, he found himself in a simple room—one table, a chair, a plant in the corner, and two doors: "Cash" and "Credit." He had no cash in his pocket, so he chose the door marked "Credit"—and found himself back on the street again.

Disillusioned, he walked back onto the construction site. Surprised that he was back so quickly, a coworker asked, "Did they fix your hand already?"

"No," he replied. "They didn't help me at all . . . but that's the most organized hospital I've ever seen!"

When it comes to his church, God is more concerned with obedience than organization, and if he had to choose between the two, I suspect he'd prefer faithful saints to functional structures.

Ultimately, this world will not be changed by well-organized church programs, magnificent church buildings, better-functioning church boards, smooth-running denominations, longer committee meetings, or the passing of more comprehensive church bylaws. These things can be useful tools for encouraging ministry, but they also can be—if we're not careful—just the opposite. These things can become obstacles to ministry that hinder our efforts to change this world for good.

This world will be changed when Christians resolve to make life, help, hope, peace, joy, truth, and love more accessible.

God, wanting to be among us and to make salvation accessible, sent Immanuel—"God with us" (Matthew 1:22-23).

To God it's all about accessibility. He has "good news that will cause great joy for all the people" (Luke 2:10). His salvation has been "prepared in the sight of all nations: a light for revelation to the Gentiles, and the glory of your people Israel" (Luke 2:30-32). God's desire has always been that "all people will see [his] salvation" (Luke 3:6). Our desires though, for the stuff of this earth, can hinder the work of evangelism and serve to make the treasures of heaven more inaccessible.

While on a mission trip to Mexico, I had the chance to tour the Metropolitan Cathedral in Mexico City. This cathedral—set in the center of a huge plaza in central Mexico City—is a magnificent structure built over three centuries. It is the oldest, and arguably the grandest, cathedral in the Americas. The interior is a breathtaking collection of gold, jewels, priceless works of art, grand marble statues, and wealth beyond my wildest imagination.

All of this stands in stark contrast to the overwhelming poverty just beyond the cathedral's doors.

The Metropolitan Cathedral was surrounded by beggars—mostly the very young and the very old—who cried out desperately for even the smallest donation. I will never forget the dirty faces of the children fighting for our attention—longing for our loose change so they could survive another day. Our tour guide said that the estimated value of the cathedral and the treasures stored in its vaults was in the billions of dollars. The contrast between the extreme wealth in that church and extreme poverty surrounding it made me sick to my stomach.

Lost, confused, and hurting people should be able to find the help they need easily, especially from the church.

That church is sitting on wealth that could change the lives of millions of people. I pray that they have a plan to help the needy people in their community, but—based on what I witnessed and the testimony of the missionaries who live and serve there—what they are doing, if anything, is making very little positive impact. From what I saw, it appears their priorities are to maintain a beautiful building, keep the tourists happy, and keep the doors of the vault locked securely.

As I toured that church building, I felt so convicted. It made me want to do more to help the people in my community. It forced me to evaluate my own church experience. I don't want to sit on God's wealth while people just outside my church doors are in need. I want to do everything I can to make God's wealth, power, and love accessible to everyone.

Lost, confused, and hurting people should be able to find the help they need easily, especially from the church. But sometimes Christians have done an extremely good job of making good help inaccessible. Although intending to be "good stewards of God's resources," sometimes Christians develop gargantuan systems through which to "freely" dispense help to the masses, systems that seem—in most cases—only to make their own lives easier, not the lives of those we are commanded to love.

Journey currently feeds fifty to seventy families a week, year-round, at a local public middle school. We've been doing this since the fall of 2009, and it all began with the vision of a young Christian woman and schoolteacher Niki Torres, who wanted to be a good steward of God's resources.

Niki called me one day at the church office and left a message. I returned her call and she asked if I'd meet with her after school the next day. I immediately said yes. I later found out that I was the only pastor who called her back.

When I arrived in Niki's classroom, I found an energetic young woman with an extraordinary vision for dispensing help to the masses of students at her school who went hungry over the weekends because their families didn't have enough money for food. More than 90 percent of the students in her school are on meal plans. In our meeting Niki mentioned that she'd recently been reminded that Jesus used food to reach people with his love and the hope of salvation.

The first edition of this book had just been released. I sat up a bit taller in my chair and asked, "So you've read my book?"

She replied, "No, I've never heard of it."

I slumped back down into my seat.

She continued, "I want to use food to minister to the kids of this school by feeding them every weekend. They don't eat over the weekends, so they come back on Mondays feeling hungry and lethargic. I have a plan."

At this point she pulled out a Walmart bag full of food that she'd purchased for just under five dollars and pointed out that a family could eat all weekend on that food. She then asked me if our church would be willing to help sponsor a few bags.

Niki looked just like Jesus to me as she shared her simple but astounding plan for making his love so accessible to his children. I said yes and told her that we'd take care of feeding all the families, immediately.

It was a no-brainer to me, such a simple way to partner with Niki to share the love of Jesus.

This is what Jesus did too. His approach was so uncomplicated. He just found lost people, loved them, and ministered to them.

As Luke points out in his Gospel, Jesus found lost people in their synagogues (4:15), in workplaces (5:27), and even in trees (19:4-5) and spent time with them. He wanted life, help, hope, peace, joy, truth, and love to be accessible, so he was accessible.

Sometimes well-intentioned Christians make it so difficult for lost people to find their way back to Jesus. If they belong to a large church, they expect people to find the service times, follow the directions on Google Maps, find an open space in the parking lot, find the right door, find the welcome center, find someone with an Ask Me badge, find their way to the nursery to drop off their child, find their way to the auditorium, find a seat that doesn't already belong to someone else, find someone to greet during the "fellowship" time, find the sermon text in the Bible, find their way to the altar, find their way back to their seat, find their way back to the nursery, find their way to their car and out of the parking lot, find their way home, and then . . . find their way back to the church building next week for the preacher's new sermon series "Seeking the Lost."

Some well-intentioned Christians may expect people to respond to the clever messages on their church signs. While on vacation in Florida, a friend of mine saw a cleverly uncompelling sign in front of his in-laws' church. The message on the homemade sign in front of the church was *supposed to be* a powerful tool for reaching lost people. As he found out, the elders of that church had instructed the deacons to make a sign to communicate to the lost people in the community that they are welcome. With the assignment clear in their heads, the deacons proceeded to make a sign with adhesive letters that read "Come, just as you are!" They put the new sign in front of the church with hopes of populating heaven, but—to their surprise—all they did was unleash the fury of hell.

One of the elders saw that sign in front of the church and blew a gasket. He called for an emergency meeting the next night. "We can't allow a sign like that to remain in front of the church!" he raged. "If we leave that sign out, telling people to come just as they are, before we know it, we'll have women showing up at church in bikinis."

Hmmm.

I need to pause here. I lived in Florida for more than thirty years, and I never saw a woman come to church in a bikini. If I had, I'd like to think that one of our greeters would have smiled, handed her a Bible, and offered her a robe. This was clearly a straw man argument.

Still, that sign was the last straw for that legalist, so he called for a vote to make the deacons fix the sign. The deacons removed the words that would have beckoned half-naked women to the steps of that church.

This is where the story gets funny, or sad, based on your perspective.

All the areas from which they had removed letters remained sticky and collected dirt as the wind blew. By the time my friend saw the sign in front of that church, a lot of dirt had collected where the old words used to be. "Come!" read the formal sign; but you could still clearly read the now banished words "just as you are!"

Talk about sending mixed messages to your community.

Talk about erecting a barrier between yourself and lost people.

We're going to discuss clothing, or the lack thereof, as a barrier to evangelism, but let me first give you a simple tool to help you not send mixed messages to the lost people in your community.

One easy thing that you and I can do to remove these barriers (if by some chance they exist at your church) is to approach the building from the parking lot on a Sunday morning and ask yourself, "If I were a first-time visitor, would I know where to go?"

Enter the building and look around. Are there greeters? Are the greeters in the right location to be the most help to you? Do you know where to drop off your kids? Are there plenty of signs to offer direction? Is the building clean? Do you know where the worship center is? Enter the children's area. Do you feel comfortable leaving your kids in this environment? Are the volunteers clearly identifiable? Are there appropriate security measures in place? Are the volunteers eager to get your child's name, or do you feel as though your child will be anonymous? Enter the auditorium. Are all the best seats taken? Do people seem eager to move and allow room for you? Were you handed a bulletin? A Bible? Do you know what's going on, or do you feel confused?

I want you to be concerned about your next-door neighbor. Do you know your next-door neighbor?

—MOTHER TERESA

As the service starts, evaluate each part as if you were a first-time guest. Do you understand the terms and procedures that are being used throughout the service? As you go through each phase of the church experience, look around with fresh eyes to see what needs to be fixed.

I've done this many times and it works.

To the Pharisees Jesus said, "You experts in the law, woe to you, because you load people down with burdens they can hardly carry, and you yourselves will not lift one finger to help them" (Luke 11:46).

Well . . . woe to misguided Christians who do the same thing. Woe to anyone who erects man-made barriers between lost people and their Savior.

Barriers such as dress codes.

CLOTHING

Woe to us if we make clothing a barrier.

Once, while celebrating the life of his friend John the baptizer, Jesus said, "Those who wear expensive clothes and indulge in luxury are in palaces" (Luke 7:25). Well, now he could easily say, "No, those who wear expensive clothes and indulge in luxury are in churches." In many places, it seems that respect for God is equated with wearing a coat and tie.

I don't hate coats and ties.

Wait . . . that's not completely true. I do actually hate ties. I'd like to meet the person who decided it is a good idea to wrap a noose around the arteries in a man's neck that lead to the brain and tighten it . . . just to cover the buttons on a shirt!

That said, I have enough social and common sense to understand the importance of dressing for success, but I also have enough Bible knowledge to know that God is not judging a fashion show. To God, "life is more than food, and the body more than clothes" (Luke 12:23). I know that "the LORD does not look at the things people look at. People look at the outward appearance, but the LORD looks at the heart" (1 Samuel 16:7).

I understand dress codes. My daughter wore a uniform to school today. I wear a dark suit to funerals, and I wear a collared shirt and long pants when I play golf. I just refuse to clothe the grace of God in a suit or a dress and require that lost men and women meet a dress code before they can meet Jesus.

Just because someone doesn't like wearing a tie to church doesn't automatically mean he doesn't love God. It might just mean that he hates ties, or he might just like breathing and the free flow of blood to the most important organ in the body!

A friend told me about a young man who couldn't wait to go to church so he could praise God with other Christians. He had just completed a six-month tour in Iraq with the navy and had much to be grateful for—three months into his mission, he'd been rescued from the ocean after being knocked off the ship. So he put on a nice polo-style shirt, a nice pair of shorts (he'd been in a uniform for six months and was ready for a break), and a pair of sandals and headed to a church.

He arrived late because he was from out of town and didn't know where he was going. The service was well underway and packed when he finally made it, so he grabbed the first available seat, in the back row next to a well-dressed older couple.

During a break in the singing, the older woman leaned over to him and whispered, "Next time you come to our church, you need to dress more appropriately."

He sat there stunned and no longer joyful.

Tears of sorrow welled up in his eyes. After sitting quietly for a few minutes, he leaned over to the woman and politely whispered, "There won't be a next time." He left the service and went back to his ship discouraged and brokenhearted.

Woe to us when we load people down with burdens they can hardly carry, such as man-made dress codes. God's dress code is simple: righteousness.

God inspired the psalmist to say, "May your priests be clothed with your righteousness; may your faithful people sing for joy" (Psalm 132:9). God inspired Isaiah to proclaim, "He has clothed me with garments of salvation and arrayed me in a robe of his righteousness" (Isaiah 61:10).

I don't care what lost people wear to church. All I care about is that they are wearing righteousness when they leave.

Another barrier we place between lost people and God may not seem to you to be a barrier at all.

CHURCH BUILDINGS

I often talk with clichés. I just can't seem to help myself. I could say, "We need to be unified as we begin this project," but instead I say, "We need to make sure we're on the same page." I could say, "I want to improve our worship service," but instead I say, "It's time to take our worship service to the next level." I could ask my team to think creatively, but it's so much more fun to ask them to "think outside the box."

To think outside the box is to see beyond the norm—to think new about something old. I'd like you to think new about the church and church buildings. I'd like you to think outside the box.

I know, I know—church buildings create identity, opportunity, stability, credibility, and reflect a commitment to the community. Church buildings are not the enemy; they are effective tools that can be used to reach people for Jesus, but they also can become—if we're not careful—big boxes that isolate Christians from the world (and each other) and sap huge amounts of time, energy, and money that could otherwise be used for outreach and staffing needs.

Please understand that I don't hate church buildings. My dad was a preacher, and I grew up sitting on the second pew on the right side of a church building. We lived in a parsonage next to a church building, so I spent countless joy-filled hours playing in a church building. I was baptized in a church building and married in a church building. I work in a church building every day. I want you to know that I don't hate church buildings, but I don't love them either—because church buildings are just very attractive, functional, but expensive tools.

Now, I know of a lot of dynamic congregations that are already thinking outside the box and effectively using their buildings to reach their world for Jesus. But there are other congregations that appear capable of thinking only *of* the box and how best to stay hidden, protected, and isolated inside their comfortable, stained-glassed world, while lost people are left to find other boxes someplace else.

Thinking outside the box about the church building is not a new concept. The first Christians did pretty well without the use of church buildings. They gathered in homes, tombs, catacombs, and anyplace else they could gather safely in the midst of persecution. A body is the image God uses for his church (Romans 12:4-5; Ephesians 5:23; Colossians 1:18), but some churches today, based on how they spend their time and money, prefer to focus on the box instead of the body.

This is problematic for several reasons.

First, boxes don't move. Boxes are not alive, so—unlike a healthy human body—they are completely immobile. The church was never meant to be viewed as an immobile box sitting on the corner of 8th and Main; God intended for us to view the church as a healthy, mobile body of believers moving—walking—through this world.

Throughout the Bible our faithfulness is compared to a walk (Psalm 1:1; 1 John 1:7). Because Jesus knows our tendency to entrench, one of his last commands to us was to go (Matthew 28:19). The church is commanded to search out and get next to lost people—to make life, help, hope,

God intended for us to view the church as a healthy, mobile body of believers moving— walking—through this world.

peace, joy, truth, and love more accessible.

I like to fish. I like to catch fish. The best way to catch fish is on a boat because a boat allows you to go wherever the fish are biting. Another way to catch fish is to build a dock and hope the fish come to you. Too many church buildings are unmovable docks—and the fish stopped biting years ago.

Second, boxes don't grow. If you've ever found yourself late on Christmas Eve trying to fit the perfect gift into an imperfect box, then you know from experience that boxes don't grow. Knowing this truth, Rick Warren used seventy-nine different facilities for functions in Saddleback Church's first fifteen years—schools, banks, recreation centers, theaters, restaurants, large homes, even a 2,300-seat tent. Warren is famous for saying, "The shoe must never tell the foot how big it can grow."[1] Healthy bodies grow, and—if we're not careful—our church boxes can hinder growth.

Third, boxes don't last. "It's all gonna burn!" We said this during a building program at a church where I served. This phrase helped us to keep the building we were going to build in proper perspective. Because of the high cost of construction and the need for a facility sufficient to support a growing congregation, we would have to spend a lot of money to build an excellent tool, but we didn't want to forget that what we were physically building was going to be temporary.

We're not the first disciples who have had to be reminded that all buildings are temporary.

Broken Bread

One of the most bonding things you can do for your own children is to care about their friends. Having four children, we have often been given the chance to provide a meal or two for their friends. Sometimes it's inconvenient, unexpected, and financially challenging (when you are already feeding a family of six), but we know these dinners are important, so we make it work.

Through these dinners we had the chance to build a relationship with one of our oldest daughter's friends, Joy, who ate dinner with us every Wednesday. Joy loved Batman, anime, and eccentric fashion. She came from a broken home and had no real ties to the father figure who lived in her house. As she ate with us, she was fed—not just food, but love, hope, and healing. The meals we shared with Joy changed our lives and hers.

—MARY—

Once, as Jesus left the Temple in Jerusalem, one of his disciples exclaimed, "Look, Teacher! What massive stones! What magnificent buildings!" To which Jesus replied, "Do you see all these great buildings? . . . Not one stone here will be left on another; every one will be thrown down" (Mark 13:1-2). And although I believe that in historical context Jesus was referring to the destruction of the Temple that was going to occur at the hand of the Romans in AD 70, his words accurately describe what the future ultimately holds for all great buildings—church buildings included.

And fourth, boxes don't care. You can't have a relationship with a building. Buildings don't walk, talk, giggle, cry, or care, but a healthy body shares both joy and pain (1 Corinthians 12:12-27). Our buildings, unless we're careful, can hinder our ministry to hurting people by distancing us from them. Jesus touched people. He listened to them, saw them, and mingled with them. If we want to be like him, then we must do everything we can to maximize the time we spend outside of our church buildings. We must be as intentional with our evangelistic efforts as possible so that we can connect with hurting people at their point—and place—of need.

Brandon does that. I first met Brandon when he was a student at Florida Christian College. I was the director of admissions, and Brandon was a ragin' Cajun from Louisiana with a passion for lost people—and for homeless people in particular. After graduation and an internship with a large homeless ministry in Atlanta, Brandon and a few friends from college started a homeless ministry in downtown Orlando. He knew that most of these people would never go to a church building, so he took the church body to them every Sunday night. Brandon understands that the way to a man's heart is truly through his stomach, so he feeds the people living under I-4 a meal before he feeds them spiritually.

He eats with sinners every Sunday night.

Brandon has made the gospel accessible, and in doing so he's had the pleasure of leading many homeless people to the Lord.

Now that's thinking outside the box!

I feel as though I need to pause here because I know what you're thinking: *Arron, out of all the possible barriers that we can put between lost people and Jesus, you chose clothes and church buildings? Are you serious? What about hypocrisy, pride, prejudice, materialism, and disunity?*

Well, those are definitely a few of the many spiritual barriers that we can put between lost people and the hope of salvation, but I wanted to identify what I think are the two biggest physical barriers, because I believe that, since they are physical, they are the easiest to deal with and a great place to start.

When people who are searching for meaning in this life encounter us, they should find hope, not hate. They should find love, not judgment. They should find us clearing a path, not cluttering it. They should find clarity, not confusion.

No one should have to wear the right clothes or walk into one of our church buildings to find life, help, hope, peace, joy, truth, and love.

No, accessing these blessings should be as easy as sitting down for a meal with you or me.

MAKING GOD'S WEALTH, POWER, AND LOVE MORE ACCESSIBLE

- Are you giving generously to God's work? Read Malachi 3:8-10. The money that you and I give to the Lord provides more resources for ministry.

- As you evaluate your own life, identify things that may be barriers between you and ministry opportunities, and take steps to remove those barriers.

- Identify ministry opportunities for yourself. God has a plan for your life and wants to use you to minister to people right where you are. Take a few moments and list some things you could do for others in the name of Jesus.

3
GRACE

All spoke well of him and were amazed at the gracious
words that came from his lips.

LUKE 4:22

I've seen the bumper sticker and I have to agree: "Mean people suck" . . . especially when they call themselves Christians.

Mean people like the members of Westboro Baptist Church in Topeka, Kansas. These people have garnered a lot of attention through their protests at prominent funerals. Their former pastor, Fred Phelps, preached that the death of soldiers in Iraq was vengeance from God for protecting a country that harbors gays. At those funeral protests, church members shouted, "God hates fags," "God hates you," and "You're going to hell" and carried signs with similar slogans.

So sad.

Their website is actually www.godhatesfags.com. I think

that domain name and everything about the Westboro Baptist Church sucks.

No wonder some people hate Christians.

Christians have been hated since the day the church began, but back then it was for the right reason: for loving Jesus. In the recent past, it seems that Christians have come to be hated not for loving Jesus too much but for loving people in the world too little. At least that's how it seems, based on what you see on TV, in Hollywood movies, and in leading newspapers. This is so unfair, because the Christians I know are loving, kind, and profoundly gracious. Unfortunately, I fear too many people perceive that Christians hate not just the sin but also the sinner.

> *Christians have come to be hated not for loving Jesus too much but for loving people in the world too little. This is so unfair.*

Philip Yancey begins *What's So Amazing about Grace?* with a story he heard from a friend who works with the down-and-out in Chicago:

> A prostitute came to me in wretched straits, homeless, sick, unable to buy food for her two-year-old daughter. Through sobs and tears, she told me she had been renting out her daughter—two years old!—to men interested in kinky sex. . . . She had to do it, she said, to support her own drug habit. I could hardly bear hearing her sordid story. . . . I had no idea what to say to this woman.

At last, I asked if she had ever thought of going to a church for help. I will never forget the look of pure, naive shock that crossed her face. "Church!" she cried. "Why would I ever go there? I was already feeling terrible about myself. They'd just make me feel worse."[1]

I spent some time watching footage of street preachers on YouTube. These graphic videos are full of yelling, arguing, and apparent hatred from the preachers to the crowds—and vice versa. A preacher on the streets of Las Vegas one New Year's Eve can be seen desperately yelling and calling people sinners as they walk by. At one point in the clip, he points at a woman in the crowd and says, "You're a bad person." Another time he points at a group of guys and says, "You guys are in serious trouble!" In another video from that night in Las Vegas, a different street preacher looking out over the crowd of people yells, "The trailer park is empty tonight!" followed by, "You are the reason why God created the lake of fire!"

What? Jesus said that God created hell "for the devil and his angels" (Matthew 25:41). God desires that no one would perish but that all would "come to repentance" (2 Peter 3:9).

I find those YouTube videos disturbing, and not because I think street preaching is wrong—the prophet Jonah preached throughout the streets of Nineveh, and the entire city repented. Some of today's street preachers may be disturbed people who need professional help; some others just need straightening out. I think their tactics are wrong.

They may—and I want to emphasize *may*—be speaking the truth, but their context is the exact opposite of a loving relationship. The best context for truth is a loving relationship, not a soap box on a street corner.

JESUS SAVES

Jesus didn't yell at lost people. He ate with lost people.

Who could hate a man who was willing to share your food, sit in your home, ignore your annoying dog, look past the stack of dishes in the sink and the pile of laundry in the corner, and proudly associate with you?

On a rusty '92 Toyota at the post office, my friend Pete saw a bumper sticker that read, "Jesus Sucks." Pete is one of the most gracious Christian men I know, but this bumper sticker made him angry, so—in a fleeting moment of ungraciousness—Pete found a marker in his car and made his way toward the Toyota to cross out the word he found so offensive. But the driver exited the post office and headed to his car at the same time.

With a jolt of nervousness mixed with righteous indignation, Pete spoke up. "I noticed your bumper sticker. I can't let you leave with that on the car."

"Are you serious?" the man asked.

"Yes, I'm serious. I find your bumper sticker incredibly offensive."

"Well, I'm not taking it off," the man replied.

Starting to calm down, Pete asked, more graciously, "Why say Jesus sucks? The only thing he's ever done for you is to die for you. You can put my name on your truck. You can even say mean things about Christians, because we sometimes screw things up, but please don't say bad things about Jesus."

The man stood speechless for a moment, and then, breaking the awkward silence, he said, "I'm not taking that bumper sticker off my car." He drove away with his opinion of Jesus still intact on his back bumper. I hope that, somewhere down the road, he'll meet other true Christ followers like Pete and change his mind about Jesus.

Jesus doesn't suck; he saves. Jesus was never mean to lost people. He was truthful but not mean. Jesus wasn't a fire-and-brimstone preacher seemingly impassioned by sending people to hell. No, he was a grace-filled Savior intent on helping people find their way to heaven.

One day, in his hometown synagogue, Jesus let everyone in on who he really was and why he was on this planet. He stood up to read, and the *chazzan* (pronounced KHAH-zahn)—the Jewish religious official who helped to conduct the service—handed him the scroll that contained a seven-hundred-year-old prophecy from Isaiah. Unrolling the scroll, Jesus began to read: "The Spirit of the Lord is on me, because he has anointed me to proclaim good news to the poor. He has sent me to proclaim freedom for the prisoners and recovery of sight for the blind, to set the oppressed free, to proclaim the year of the Lord's favor" (Luke 4:18-19; see also Isaiah 61:1-2).

When he stopped reading, he rolled up the scroll, handed it back to the chazzan, and sat down. In the synagogue the rabbis didn't teach standing up, so when Jesus sat down, he wasn't finished—he was just getting started.

Jesus waited for every eye to fix on him. He waited for the next teachable moment. Then he started his lesson with eight simple words announcing one amazing message: "Today this scripture is fulfilled in your hearing" (Luke 4:21).

Whoa!

Jesus was telling them that he was the Messiah whose coming had been anticipated. Their waiting was over. They were living in the year of the Lord's favor!

> *All spoke well of [Jesus] and were amazed at the gracious words that came from his lips.*
> —LUKE 4:22

Luke recorded, "All spoke well of him and were amazed at the gracious words that came from his lips" (Luke 4:22). Gracious words. Jesus spoke words extending undeserved favor, love, mercy, and hope—God's grace.

As God, Jesus knew that in about two minutes the crowd was going to try to throw him off the nearest cliff (Luke 4:29). So he could have said, "You think you have me all figured out, but you're clueless. In about one minute I'm going to remind you that God sent Elijah, not to the Jewish widows in Israel, but to a Gentile widow in Zarephath—and it's going to make you angry. And then, about two seconds after that I'm going to remind you that God sent Elisha, not to the lepers in Israel, but to a Gentile leper named Naaman—and you're going to flip your lids. You jerks! You say you love me, but you hate Gentiles and that's not how it works. If you really loved me, you'd love Gentiles too. So when you try to execute me—it's on! I'm going to call down some serious fire on your nasty little heads!"

But that's not what Jesus did.

Even knowing that they were going to try to kill him momentarily, he was not mean. He was kind and spoke words full of grace that gave hope to the poor.

GOOD NEWS TO THE POOR

Poor people need good news, and there are a lot of financially poor people in this world. If the whole world consisted of only one hundred people, forty-three would be living without basic sanitation, twenty-one would be struggling to live on $1.25 a day or less, and twenty people would have 75 percent of the world's wealth.[2]

If you are a citizen living in the United States, you live in the richest country in the world, yet according to US census data, about 43.1 million people here live in poverty.[3]

Jesus cared about financially poor people. He didn't yell "Get a job!" as he drove past. He didn't look the other way when he saw them standing next to his car at a stoplight, holding a cardboard "Will work for food" sign. He never believed they were getting what they deserved, because he knew they deserved so much more.

Jesus, God incarnate, knew that poor people deserved justice:

> I know how many are your offenses and how great
> your sins. There are those who oppress the innocent
> and take bribes and deprive the poor of justice in the
> courts.
>
> AMOS 5:12

Jesus knew that poor people deserved protection:

> Do not oppress the widow or the fatherless, the
> foreigner or the poor.
> ZECHARIAH 7:10

Jesus knew that poor people deserved shelter and provision:

> Is not this the kind of fasting I have chosen: to loose
> the chains of injustice and untie the cords of the
> yoke, to set the oppressed
> free and break every yoke? Is
> it not to share your food with
> the hungry and to provide the
> poor wanderer with shelter—
> when you see the naked, to clothe them, and not to
> turn away from your own flesh and blood?
> ISAIAH 58:6-7

Jesus cared about financially poor people. He didn't yell "Get a job!" as he drove past.

Jesus knew that poor people—people who were both financially and spiritually poor—deserved the Kingdom:

> Blessed are you who are poor, for yours is the
> kingdom of God.
> LUKE 6:20

Jesus knew that poor people deserved a seat at his banquet
table.

> When you give a banquet, invite the poor, the
> crippled, the lame, the blind, and you will be
> blessed.
>
> LUKE 14:13-14

What do you believe that poor people deserve?

Chris was poor. I met him through Brandon's street ministry (described in chapter 2), but I got to know him over lunch at McDonald's. He and I came from different worlds. He is black. I am white. He has no family. I have a large family. He is broke. I'm not.

As we ate together, I also discovered that he and I came from the same world. He was a sinner in need of grace, and I am a sinner saved by grace. Leading him to the Lord over the next week was a wonderful experience. He's not spiritually poor anymore, and—thanks to Brandon—he's on the path to escaping financial poverty as well.

If you're honest, you might have to admit that most of the time you think poor people are a nuisance. I'm a preacher, and we preachers can be the worst offenders. Preachers have "important" things to do, and honestly, it can be annoying to be trying to finish my sermon on service only to have my admin call to say there's a benevolence case waiting for me in the reception area! So we usher the poor away quickly with a can of Vienna sausages, an oatmeal pie, a pat on the back, and directions to the shelter downtown.

Shame on us.

Shame on me.

That's not a very nice way to treat poor people.

You might be thinking that there are a lot of people who try to take advantage of churches, and we need to be good stewards of God's money; it makes sense to send poor people to a facility (like a shelter) where they can receive more than a can of food from the pantry next to the church broom closet. I've had those same thoughts, but I also know that one of the reasons Jesus came into this world was to share Good News with poor people and that he expects us to invite them to the banquet. And when we invite them, he wants us to use gracious words.

FREEDOM FOR THE PRISONERS

According to data provided by the Bureau of Justice Statistics, more than 6.8 million men and women in the United States are incarcerated or under the supervision of probation officers. That means that one out of every thirty-six Americans is not free.[4]

There are countless people imprisoned by fear, addiction, abuse, and guilt, and we must tell them that they can be free.

I believe that Jesus wants all people to find salvation— including prisoners who are incarcerated for breaking the law—but I think Jesus' application of Isaiah's prophecy in the synagogue has a broader application than that.

During the time in which Isaiah prophesied, Judah was invaded by Syria and Ephraim in 734 BC; then it happened again at the hands of King Sennacherib and the Assyrians thirty-three years later. Sennacherib's invasion resulted in brutal treatment of God's people, but as terrible as the

Assyrian invasion was, the worst was yet to come—Judah would be held captive in Babylon, where the people and their descendants would remain for about seventy years.

Isaiah's prophecy was spoken to give God's imprisoned people the hope that one day they would be free again.

Jesus referenced Isaiah's prophecy seven hundred years later in that synagogue in Nazareth to give God's imprisoned people—and all other people held captive against their wills—the hope that they would be free again . . . not one day . . . but today! "*Today* this scripture is fulfilled in your hearing" (Luke 4:21, emphasis added).

Today, in our world, there are countless people imprisoned by fear, addiction, abuse, and guilt, and we must tell them that they can be free. Some of them may feel as though they are getting what they deserve. Some of them may hear condemnatory sermons decrying their situations, leading them to believe that God thinks they are getting what they deserve.

We can do better. We must do better proclaiming freedom for the prisoners in our world.

For some, freedom feels like an illusion. But to Harry Houdini, master illusionist, escape artist, and international phenomenon, captivity was the true illusion. Legend has it that when Houdini was at the height of his career, he would arrive at a city to perform, but first he would challenge local police to restrain him with shackles and lock him in their jails. One time Houdini almost lost the challenge. Left alone in a cell, he took the cuffs off easily, but for some reason he couldn't pick the lock on the cell door. About to give up in frustration, Houdini leaned against the door, and it opened. The guards had forgotten to lock it.

We must let the captives around us know that their prison door is not really locked. It's merely a trick that a master illusionist, Satan, is using to shackle them with hopelessness and despair. We must let the captives around us know that Jesus, the Way, has arrived and is speaking a gracious word that will change their lives: *freedom*.

SIGHT FOR THE BLIND

In 1989 the *New York Times* reported that David St. John, a blind man, was beaten by police officers who said they thought his folding white cane was a martial arts weapon. He said the officers did not identify themselves, and he thought he was being mugged.[5] It's bad enough for a visually impaired man to be beaten up, but it's even more terrible when this happens at the hands of those who are charged with protecting him.

Through Moses, God made it clear that physically blind people were to be protected: "Cursed is anyone who leads the blind astray on the road" (Deuteronomy 27:18). Jesus also cared about physically blind people, healing many of them throughout his ministry. He was even more concerned with those who were spiritually blind, because spiritual blindness, unlike physical blindness, keeps people from seeing heaven.

Jesus wants spiritually blind people to see, and he wants Christians to see the spiritually blind. We don't always see people. We rush by them as if they don't exist or matter in our world. Like the poor, spiritually blind people can be annoying. They often require a significant investment of our time to help them find their way. Their ignorance of deep spiritual realities may frustrate us. Their spiritual blindness may lead them into harmful paths that require someone to rescue them. But don't let that deter you from helping them find their way home. Remember, they have never truly seen, and they are trying to grasp about in darkness.

They must make it home. We must help them make it home so they can take their place at our Father's banquet table.

RELEASE FOR THE OPPRESSED

Bono, lead singer for the rock band U2, has always had a love for the oppressed. As an activist in the fight against poverty, he is leading the effort to cure AIDS and to care for those suffering from HIV. For his passion to release those who are oppressed by abusive regimes or devastating diseases, Bono has been nominated multiple times for the Nobel Peace Prize.

Bono believes that today is the day to end oppression, that this is the year of the Lord's favor. This is good news and it must be shared—but it must be shared graciously. In an article in *Relevant* magazine, Bono revealed that encounters with some ungracious evangelicals had led him to harbor a poor opinion of the church, but that—over time—his opinion of the church has completely changed: "I kind of thought the Church was asleep and it turned into a 'holy-bless-me club' or whatever you want to call it, [but] I'm glad to say

I was wrong," he admitted. "Particularly evangelicals, who seemed very judgmental to me over the years, turned out to be incredibly generous in their time and their support of this effort. I've really had my view of the Church turned upside down. . . . It's [also] given me great faith in the Church. I have always had it in God."[6]

I long for people to have faith in both God and the church, so I long for the church to graciously proclaim a message of hope to all lost people. As we seek to build relationships with lost people by inviting them to the table, we must do so with hearts full of love and words full of grace.

Jesus was full of grace. He had the heart of a loving Savior, not of an angry street preacher. Isaiah prophesied about Jesus: "He will not shout or cry out, or raise his voice in the streets. A bruised reed he will not break, and a smoldering wick he will not snuff out" (Isaiah 42:2-3).

I want the woman who feels like a bruised reed—ready to break in half and give up—to know that she is safe with Jesus.

I want the lonely and hurting man who feels like the flame of his soul is about to be snuffed out to know that Jesus stands waiting to rekindle the fire.

I want that prostitute who allowed her daughter to be sexually abused to know that there is hope. There is another—a better—way, and Jesus stands ready not to send her to hell but to help her and her daughter find their way to heaven.

And I want the angry man with the "Jesus Sucks" bumper sticker to know that Jesus wants nothing more than to put a loving arm around his shoulder while whispering graciously in his ear, "It's okay. I forgive you."

SHOWING GRACE IN PRACTICAL WAYS

· Do you have a plan to help the poor people you encounter? Does your church have a plan? Make a plan that involves connecting poor people with professional relief agencies, job training, faith-based counseling, and lasting support. Identify ways to help that involve more than handing over cash. Secure gas vouchers, gift certificates for grocery stores (make sure these can't be used to buy alcohol), bus passes. Research a process for paying bills directly for the person in need. If you see poor people regularly on your daily commute, you might consider carrying a small cooler in your car. Stock it with bottled water, sealed fruit cups, apples, and other items that can be easily dispensed. Other items that don't need to be cooled are granola bars, oatmeal pies, pop-open cans of meat or fruit, candy bars, and snack crackers.

· If your church doesn't already have a prison ministry, find out what it would take to start one. You may also consider getting approved by the law-enforcement officials in your county to be a regular visitor and/or counselor in your local jail. Remember the prisoners' families: Contact the local jail ministry to learn what you can do to minister to the children of the prisoners in their facility. Christmas toy drives and care packages are great ways to minister to these children.

· Contact an organization that serves visually impaired people in your community and offer to read the Bible or daily devotionals with anyone needing that service. You may also find that your local nursing home has visually impaired people who would love to have someone read the Bible to them. Are you willing to give a visually impaired person a ride to church? Does your church have a van or a bus? Set up a ministry. Some visually impaired people don't go to church simply because they don't have a way to get there.

4
FAITH

Put out into deep water, and
let down the nets for a catch.

LUKE 5:4

There are no lost causes.

Just ask Mange Ram.

In August 2008, nineteen-year-old Mange Ram of India was on a religious pilgrimage with hundreds of other people. Rumors of a landslide swept through the crowd, triggering a stampede. Panicked people began trampling one another to get to safety. Ram was knocked down, which is the last thing he remembers before losing consciousness. The next thing Ram remembers is waking up as doctors were preparing to perform his autopsy!

Nearly 150 people died in the stampede. Rescue workers, in an attempt to clear the path so the pilgrimage could continue, rapidly gathered the bodies, piled them up, and shipped them off to the morgue, where Ram awoke.

"When I woke up," he said, "I was in the middle of a row of bodies waiting for postmortem. . . . My throat was parched and I asked for water. Towering over me the doctors and nursing staff . . . looked dazed. They must have been surprised to see a dead man come alive like that."[1]

Have you ever felt as though everyone has given up on you? As if you've been prematurely taken to the morgue for an autopsy?

Before his death last year, Gary Hamilton was a dear friend and an elder at the church where I'm blessed to serve. In his thirties Gary was a man people looked up to. When he walked into a room, people noticed. As a successful young farmer on a large farm, he was well known in his northern Colorado farming community. He was popular, but despite having a wife and kids, he was also very lonely. Looking for a way to escape his feelings of desperation and emptiness, he began spending nights at local bars, drinking heavily and using drugs.

On what he eventually came to call a suicide mission, Gary indulged in risky behaviors that led to several run-ins with law enforcement. His last run-in with the law sent him to prison for twelve years for possession of drugs and a sawed-off shotgun.

Inside the prison Gary felt like a lost cause, as though he'd been left for dead. He lost his farm, his reputation, and his hope. Depressed and broken, Gary planned on killing himself when the first opportunity presented itself. He thought he had messed up too much to be of any good to anyone, so he was surprised when a stranger took an interest in him.

Rick, a volunteer for Chuck Colson's Prison Fellowship, visited Gary's cell only three days after Gary began serving his sentence. Rick invited him to a Bible study, but Gary replied, "I don't need a Bible study. All I need is a way out of here," meaning a way to kill himself. Unfazed by Gary's response, Rick offered to bring Gary a Bible and promised that he would return with one shortly.

Gary didn't think he'd see Rick again, but Rick came right back with a Bible. Gary began to read it, and the message he read was clear: With God there's always a way, with God there's always a hope, and with God there's always a chance.

That night, after reading the Bible for several hours, Gary thought, *Just maybe everything Kathy has been telling me is true.* Gary's wife, Kathy, was a strong Christian who had been witnessing to Gary for years. In the darkness of his prison cell, Gary was starting to see the Light for the very first time. That night he got on his knees and prayed, "Lord, if you're real, please make yourself real to me."

The cell was pitch black, but Gary felt as if it lit up as God made his presence known and Gary experienced release from the garbage of his life. He immediately got involved in two Bible studies a week. He couldn't get enough of God, and he couldn't stop telling the other inmates about what God had done for him. He eventually led many of them to Jesus. Gary was a new creation who felt reborn and—for the first time in many decades—hopeful.

One day Jesus was fishing for men on the shores of the

Sea of Galilee. He saw two boats sitting at the water's edge as the fishermen washed their nets after a night of fishing. Jesus wasn't close to being done—he was just getting started—so he got in the boat that belonged to Simon Peter and asked Peter to put it out a little from shore (Luke 5:1-3).

With God there's always a way, with God there's always a hope, and with God there's always a chance.

Jesus is an amazing fisher of men. He knows the best bait to use. He understands people's behavioral patterns, and he knows all the best places to reach them. Jesus knew that if he wanted to catch the hearts of the most people, he needed to get out onto the water so they could hear him better. Jesus used the Sea of Galilee like an amphitheater; the water helped people hear the sound of his voice.

When he was finished speaking, Jesus told Peter, "Put out into deep water, and let down the nets for a catch" (Luke 5:4). Now, most of the fishermen I know are reluctant to give up their secrets unless they're forced to. Jesus was eager to share what he knew about catching fish. In his instructions to Simon Peter, he revealed two secrets to successful fishing for fish and for men: faith ("put out into deep water") and action ("let down the nets for a catch").

PUT OUT INTO DEEP WATER

Too often we like to play it safe.

While working in Yellowstone National Park, I saw a lot of wonderful things, but I also saw some odd things. One of the odd sights I saw regularly was someone fishing for trout on the side of the road in a pond formed by melted snow. To the novice, that looked like a nice little trout pond, but anyone with any experience with northern fishing knows that the only thing a small pond on the side of a road will yield is a small trout—and only if the pond is more than a temporary puddle caused by melted snow. The big trout can best be reached by being waist deep in raging, ice-cold water in the heart of the wilderness.

Big fish typically live in the deep water, and lost souls often live in "the deep" too. If you and I want to catch big spiritual fish, we're going to have to go deeper.

Deeper into the heart of the inner city. Get involved with an inner-city mission.

Deeper into the counterculture. Join clubs that will help you meet a variety of people in your community.

Deeper into the world of entertainment. Use your talents in filmmaking, acting, and screenwriting.[2]

Deeper into government. Run for office.

Deeper into the bar scene. Ask the local bar owner if you can start a Saturday morning Bible study at the bar. Make yourself available to drive drunk people home on a weekend night.

Deeper into the public-school system. Become a teacher, join the local school board, or get involved in the PTA.

Deeper into the world.

How often are our evangelistic efforts akin to fishing in a puddle of snowmelt? If we evaluated what some churches are spending on reaching the lost and what they are actually doing to reach the lost, it's the equivalent of sticking our heads out of the front doors of our sanctuaries—just beyond the earshot of sinners, whispering the name of Jesus, and then weeping because more lost people aren't responding to the gospel.

They aren't responding to the gospel because we aren't responding to the gospel.

Jesus clearly commanded us to go deep "into all the world and preach the gospel to all creation" (Mark 16:15). But like pathetic fishermen standing ankle deep in snowmelt, too many of us have chosen safety and convenience over risk and inconvenience, and we are never going to catch anything . . . unless we go deeper.

Jesus wanted Peter to experience a huge catch, so he sent him to deep waters to find it . . . and to find bigger faith.

I've yet to meet a great fisherman who is not also a person of great faith. Great fishermen fish because they believe that they are just about to catch the next fish. This faith keeps them fishing.

I've yet to meet a person of great faith who is not also a great fisherman—not for fish but for souls. People of faith believe that they are just about to reach the next person for Jesus. This faith keeps them fishing.

When Jesus told Peter to put his boat in deep water, Peter's faith in fishing for that day was faltering at best. He had fished all night. His first response gave a reason why it wasn't going to work: "Master, we've worked hard all night and haven't caught anything" (Luke 5:5).

Linear thinking is an enemy to faith.

My simple definition of linear thinking is "drawing conclusions about the immediate future based on the immediate past," which is what Peter was doing and what we often do too. Peter's immediate past experience on the water wasn't good. Peter and his friends had worked hard fishing all night, and they hadn't caught anything; therefore, it was logical—at least to Peter—that they weren't going to catch any more fish a few short hours later. The fish just weren't biting. Peter believed that fishing that day was a lost cause.

I've yet to meet a person of great faith who is not also a great fisherman—not for fish but for souls.

But Jesus believes in lost causes. No one or no situation is too far gone to be saved, as long as Jesus is around. Jesus wanted Peter—and us—to have more faith.

Linear thinking says cancer always wins, but faith disagrees. Linear thinking says most marriages end in divorce, but faith disagrees. Linear thinking says bankruptcy is the only option, but faith disagrees. Linear thinking says rebellious teens don't change, but faith disagrees. Linear thinking says the fish aren't biting, but faith disagrees.

Linear thinking says there is no hope for the prostitute, the abusive alcoholic, the adulterous spouse, the murderer, and the northern Colorado farmer convicted of dealing drugs, but faith disagrees—because with Jesus there are no lost causes.

Thank goodness Peter had enough respect for Jesus to be

Do you know how this world would be changed if we simply did what Jesus told us to do, simply because he said so?

willing to give it one more try: "Because you say so, I will let down the nets" (Luke 5:5). Do you know how this world would be changed if we simply did what Jesus told us to do, simply because he said so?

Because Jesus said so, Peter put his faith into action and let down his nets.

LET DOWN THE NETS FOR A CATCH

I learned one of my most important fishing lessons the first time I went fishing with Grandpa Chambers. Grandpa drove his fishing boat to his secret fishing hole, killed the engine, and told my brother and me what to do to catch fish. I followed his advice exactly . . . almost. I hooked the bait the way he said and held my pole the way he said, but I wasn't catching anything. I didn't know why until Grandpa uttered these wise and important words: "You aren't going to catch any fish unless you put your bait in the water."

In my excitement to be fishing with Grandpa, I had forgotten to cast my line into the water.

It's one thing to want to catch fish; it's another thing to put your bait in the water.

It's one thing to have faith in Jesus and put out into deep water; it's another to put your faith into action and let down the nets for a catch.

Throughout the Bible we see people combining faith and action.

Noah proved his faith in God by building a boat and putting his family into it (Genesis 6:13-22).

Abraham proved his faith in God by building an altar and putting Isaac on it (Genesis 22:6-10).

Moses proved his faith in God by facing his fears and facing Pharaoh (Exodus 7:1-7).

The Israelites proved their faith in God by walking around Jericho once a day for six days and seven times on the seventh day, shouting at Joshua's command while the priests blew their trumpets (Joshua 6).

A man born blind proved his faith in Jesus by washing the mud off his eyes in the pool of Siloam (John 9:1-7).

Peter proved his faith in Jesus by getting out of the boat and walking toward Jesus on the water (Matthew 14:22-29).

We prove our faith in God by putting our faith into action. James said, "As the body without the spirit is dead, so faith without deeds is dead" (James 2:26). As we eat with sinners, we must have faith that God wants to save them. We must also be willing to do whatever it takes to make sure they know that.

Peter followed Jesus' command, putting his faith into action and his nets into the water, and the results were overwhelming.

ASTONISHING BLESSINGS

The blessings that come from fishing are evident on the days when you catch your limit: the cooler is full, the bugs aren't biting, the lake is calm, and a delicious fish dinner is in your future. But sometimes the fish just aren't biting, and all you want to do is clean your nets and call it a day.

Fishing with Jesus is like the first kind of day. Jesus, the master fisherman, knows how to catch fish because he knows fish, so when you fish with Jesus the blessings are astonishing.

When Jesus told Peter to put out to deep water and let down the nets, he also promised him fish. He said, "Let down the nets for a catch" (Luke 5:4).

Did you get that? The fish were waiting; the blessing was guaranteed.

When Peter followed Jesus' instructions, he caught so many fish that the nets began to break. He had to call his partners, James and John, to come and help him, and the fish so filled the boats that they both began to sink. Luke wrote that Peter and his companions were "astonished at the catch of fish they had taken" (Luke 5:9).

Wouldn't it be wonderful if you and the disciples in your church reached so many lost people for Jesus that the walls of your building began to crumble from the number of those crammed in? Wouldn't it be great to be astonished by the number of people coming to Jesus through the relationships you built while eating with them?

Amazing things happen in the world of fishing all the time. Just ask David Hayes of North Carolina.

David's granddaughter was fishing with him, when she asked him to hold her pink Barbie rod and reel while she went to the restroom. He did. When the bobber suddenly went underwater, he realized that a fish had just taken the bait—a big fish. After a thirty-minute battle, David landed a state-record channel catfish weighing twenty-one pounds, one ounce![3] Wow!

"The Jackson 5" on I-95

A sunny day on the east coast of Florida. I was heading southbound with a friend, a paramedic. Not more than thirty minutes into the trip, we topped an overpass and there to the side of the road, a van lay quietly crumpled on its side, like an aluminum can discarded by a passing motorist. Inside the vehicle a family of five from Maryland, named Jackson, was in shock. A passing car had gotten too close to the Jackson vehicle, and in an attempt to create space, Mr. Jackson overcompensated—resulting in his car careening down an embankment and doing a complete rollover. It could have been a lost cause.

We were the first people on the scene, so my friend and I did what we could to help. When emergency personnel arrived, Mr. Jackson was taken to a local hospital.

Later that evening, we visited with him and helped his family find local housing. Our church provided them with care, food, and the love of Jesus, and during this time we were able to share the gospel with the family.

The Jacksons eventually headed home to Maryland. I kept in contact with the family and connected them with a church in their area. Eight months—to the day—after their accident, I received a call from Mrs. Jackson. "I'm coming back to Florida to see you," she said, "and I want to talk with you more about the Lord. Are you open?"

"Anytime!" I responded. Five days and a forty-five-minute conversation later, we saw two members of that family make a commitment to Jesus, and as we raised them out of the waters of baptism, Mrs. Jackson said, "It took an accident on a Florida road to get my life on the right one. God is good!"

—SCOTT—

Amazing things happen all the time for Christians who are fishing for lost people too. If you and I will put our faith into action as we fish for people, we will experience astonishing blessings. But that's not all. We also will find a higher purpose.

HIGHER PURPOSE

Jesus had an uncommon plan for these common fishermen, a special job he wanted them to do. So he said to Peter, "Don't be afraid; from now on you will fish for people" (Luke 5:10). Imagine how exhilarating this had to be in the context of what had just happened. Peter and his companions were probably still breathing heavily and slapping high fives as they celebrated the amazing catch of fish. These guys fished for a living. This catch of fish was sure to be a huge financial blessing and change their lives—at least for the near future—so they did what any of us would have done. They immediately began to process the fish so they could be sold at the nearest market. Right?

Wouldn't it be wonderful if you and the disciples in your church reached so many lost people for Jesus that the walls of your building began to crumble from the number of those crammed in?

Wrong! That's not what they did at all.

Luke tells us that they "left everything and followed" Jesus (Luke 5:11). They left two boatfuls of fish on the shore to follow Jesus so they could start fishing for lost people. But they also left their livelihood—two boats and all their nets—and their homes and families (Mark 10:28-30) to follow Jesus. We assume they checked in on their families, provided for them, and stayed with them at times—but they were students of Jesus, and in that day, the students stayed with the teacher.

These fishermen had seen what Jesus could do when they put their simple faith into action, so when he offered them a higher purpose for their lives, they eagerly accepted his offer. It was a classic example of catch and release. Jesus caught these men on the water's edge so that he could release them with a higher purpose: to catch other lost people with the gospel.

God has a higher purpose for our lives too. He caught us so that he could release us into this world to catch lost people who feel as though they've been left for dead . . . people like my friend Gary.

Upon his release from prison, Gary knew that God had a higher purpose for his life, so he immediately devoted himself to growing in Jesus and being a man of God in his home and in his community. He began to share his faith in Jesus and his testimony with anyone who would listen. Prison Fellowship hired Gary to be the director of their ministries in northern Colorado, Wyoming, and Montana.

At a woman's prison in Montana, Gary met a woman who was on death row for murdering her parents. She told Gary that she felt like a lost cause. Gary told her that—with God— there are no lost causes. Through an intentional relationship developed over a long period of time, Gary introduced this woman to Jesus Christ and told her of the hope that all can have through him. The woman listened, believed, accepted Jesus, and found life on death row.

Five years after he left prison, Gary and his wife were in an accident in which their car was hit by a train. Gary's wife died instantly, and Gary was left paralyzed from the chest down.

Although his heart and body were broken, Gary's faith was completely intact. Even from his hospital bed, he continued to share the gospel with anyone who would listen and he did so until his death. Gary was a man of great faith, so—though he was paralyzed and in a wheelchair—people still looked up to him when he entered a room.

Did I tell you that Gary was a world-class fisherman and outdoorsman? He could catch anything, anywhere, anytime. He devoted a significant amount of time to organizing trips for special-needs kids, to teach them how to fish.

Now, I never went fishing with Gary on one of those trips, but based on what I know of Gary and the deep faith he had, I know what he told the kid who was sad and ready to give up because he wasn't catching any fish. I bet you he encouraged the child by saying, "Don't quit. There are no lost causes. Let's 'put out into deep water, and let down the nets for a catch.'"

GOING DEEPER INTO THE WORLD

- Identify one local mission with whom you can work to reach people with specific needs. Get involved to make a difference in your community.

- Identify a foreign mission that you can support financially, spiritually, or physically (by going), and partner with them in changing the world.

5
INTIMACY

Why do you eat and drink with
tax collectors and sinners?

LUKE 5:30

Intimacy. This word evokes different images in the minds of men and women.

Many women envision taking long walks in the rain, having conversations over candlelight in which deep feelings are verbalized (men, that means "with words"), listening to Adele music, holding hands, laughing together, crying together, sitting together, reading in the same room together, working in the yard together, playing with the kids together, and doing pretty much anything together.

I don't think most men know what intimacy really means. To many men, intimacy evokes images of . . . well . . . um . . . uh . . . you know, and definitely not the kind of thing a

Christian man should be involved in with a neighbor. So it's a good thing that that's not the kind of intimacy I'm talking about.

Men (and women, but especially men): The word *intimacy* means so much more than you may think it does and is so much more important to evangelism than most of us seem to realize.

To Jesus, the word *intimacy* evoked images of eating and drinking with sinners. Eating with someone in the first century was an intimate act. Eating with someone in the ancient world was a statement, not just an act of hospitality. When people ate with others in the time of Jesus, they were stating that they were willing to be connected with—and that they accepted—the individual or group with whom they were eating.

The word "intimacy" means so much more than you may think it does and is so much more important to evangelism than most of us seem to realize.

This practice of Jesus—being intimate with sinners—was one of the biggest reasons Jesus was criticized by the Pharisees and teachers of the law. In his book *The Ragamuffin Gospel,* Brennan Manning explained why: "In first-century Palestinian Judaism the class system was enforced rigorously. It was legally forbidden to mingle with sinners who were outside the law: table fellowship with beggars, tax collectors . . . and prostitutes was religiously, socially, and culturally taboo." Manning wrote that in the Near East today, "an Orthodox Jew's saying 'I would like to have dinner with you' is a metaphor that implies, 'I would like to enter into friendship with you.'"[1]

When Jesus ate with people, he was committing an act of intimacy.

My friend and associate minister, Terry Davis, committed an act of intimacy with a guy at the gym named Brendon. Let me tell you that story, but first, let me pause here and make an important point: One of the most effective tools you have in sharing your faith is simply your story. Just share what Jesus has done for you, and you'll be sharing the story of salvation.

Let me tell you what God did for Brendon through Terry.

Brendon is a very muscular man. He's what they call huge! He's also covered in tattoos and walks around the gym like some sort of Frankenstein. Terry and I work out at the same gym where Brendon works out, and Brendon works out all the time, so we both saw Brendon regularly. Yet I was afraid of Brendon, so I avoided him.

Just share what Jesus has done for you, and you'll be sharing the story of salvation.

Not so with Terry. Terry never saw Brendon as a lost cause, so he went out of his way to talk to Brendon and build a relationship with him.

Because Terry actually spent time getting to know Brendon, he found out that Brendon walked as he did because he was technically paralyzed. Brendon was in a horrible motorcycle accident about ten years ago and almost died. If it hadn't been for the quick actions of a woman who now works at Journey, Janet Morris, who was in a car right behind the accident and jumped out to perform CPR, Brendon would have died. He didn't die, but he was paralyzed and now can only walk because his legs are stiff and act like crutches.

Brendon walked away from that accident and his months in the hospital with anger toward God. He wanted nothing to do with God and Christians, so he ignored Terry for two weeks after he found out that Terry was a minister. Terry didn't give up on Brendon and, like true north, stayed true in his love for and commitment to him.

Eventually Brendon started talking to Terry again, and their relationship grew deeper and deeper. Terry found out that Brendon played professional sled hockey for the Colorado Avalanche and that they were having a tournament in Denver. Terry and his family went to Denver for a weekend to watch Brendon play and cheer for him. After that weekend, Brendon told Terry how much he appreciated that they came and noted that his live-in girlfriend had never come to one of his games.

Fast-forward a few months. Terry knew that Brendon and his girlfriend were living together and that all relationships can use some help, so he invited Brendon to a men's retreat at Journey. Brendon first said no but eventually said yes and showed up. He took pages of notes on how to be a man of God. He then shocked us all by showing up at our first service the next day and then shocked us even more by staying for all three morning services! Brendon didn't miss a church service for close to six months.

One Monday, Brendon called the office and asked to speak with me and Terry. Brendon showed up and told us that he'd prayed on the way to church the day before and asked God to prove his love for him.

Brendon said that in my sermon I specifically said "God

loves you" several times. I don't remember saying it once. He said that when he got in the car after church, the song on the radio was "He loves us, oh, how he loves us." When he got home he sat down in front of the TV. As he flipped the channels he turned to a Christian station just as the preacher on stage at some church somewhere was saying, "Some of you just need to know God loves you."

Brendon got the message. He hit his knees and told God that he now believed God loved him and that he wanted to give his life to Jesus.

As Terry and I listened with knowing smiles on our faces, he said, "I just wanted you guys to know that I think I'm a Christian now!" We all laughed, hugged, and made plans for his baptism. After a few months Brendon informed us that due to lifestyle differences, he and his girlfriend of six years had parted ways. We all hugged again and praised God for grace, forgiveness, and the way he worked powerfully through Terry and Brendon's relationship.

One dictionary definition of *intimacy* is "marked by a very close association." I'm convinced that God used Terry to reach Brendon through a very close association and that God is using Brendon now to reach the people of Guatemala through his mission work there.

Jesus was marked for criticism—and ultimately death—because of his very close association with people whom the Pharisees and teachers of the law felt compelled to keep outside the fence. The Pharisees and teachers of the law believed they existed to identify and protect the barriers they had erected in the name of the Mosaic law. Jesus was no respecter of their man-made barriers—and that made him a threat.

Writing on the subject, Santos Yao, a Christian minister in the Greater Los Angeles area, noted, "Jesus . . . violated the sacred social boundaries of the Jewish community thus prompting the Jewish leaders to insist on his destruction."[2]

Is Yao right? Did the leaders of the Jewish community really want to kill Jesus because he ate with sinners?

Yes.

How could they hate Jesus that much? How could they hate sinners that much?

The Jewish community in Jesus' time was group oriented. One's identity and place in society were determined by the group with whom one belonged. The group took precedence over the individual, so protecting the Jewish group was of primary importance. The way the Jewish community saw things, "likes eat with likes."[3] When Jesus ate with sinners, such as Levi and the other tax collectors (Luke 5:27-32), he wasn't just saying "I like you" or "I am with you." He was saying, "I am you" (John 1:14; Philippians 2:7).

That's the ultimate blessing of the incarnation and a mystery too many don't understand. Jesus didn't just come to visit us; he came to become one of us. He was all God, yet still all human.

In fact, if he were here today, you'd probably see him at the Waffle House late at night, and he'd be able to tell you the name of every server and how long each has worked there.

He'd enjoy sitting with you on your porch and talking about the weather. He'd cry with you when he hears about your miscarriage. He'd celebrate with you on your thirtieth wedding anniversary.

He'd sit at your dinner table and compliment your pot roast, even though you both know it's a little dry. Yes, he'd eat with you and me because we're his kind of people.

His kind of people—the people with whom Jesus mostly ate—were viewed by the Jewish community as being of a lower class, a different group. The peasant farmers, crafts-men, day laborers, tax collectors, and all others who belonged to this lower class were known as the *am-ha-'aretz*—"people of the soil." A rule among the rabbis warned, "The disciples of the learned shall not recline at table in the company of the 'am-ha-'aretz."[4]

Remember, "likes eat with likes." Levi and his tax-collector friends were definitely "people of the soil," but Jesus didn't care. He accepted Levi, and Levi in turn accepted Jesus and threw a banquet in his honor, which made the legalists mad. "Why do you eat and drink with tax collectors and sinners?" they asked (Luke 5:30).

Good question.

Jesus ate with tax collectors and sinners because, unlike the Pharisees, teachers of the law, and some Christians, he wanted to have an intimate relationship with all sinners—including us. I think this passage (Luke 5:27-32) reveals three of the barriers to true intimacy.

"EXCEPTANCE"

Never heard of exceptance? Well, that's because I made it up. (It says in the Writers' Employee Manual that we are allowed to make up words if we have to.) *Exceptance* is basically the opposite of *acceptance*.

The Pharisees and teachers of the law could not understand why Jesus would *accept* a man like Levi on his team. When Jesus said to Levi, "Follow me" (Luke 5:27), he shocked the religious leaders, because Levi was exactly the type of person they *excepted*—excluded.

I must confess that there are a few people in this world I'd have no problem excepting. I have a short list. The problem is—if I read the Bible correctly—we Christians are not allowed to except anyone. Exceptance is not permissible for us, but it was definitely practiced by the four largest Jewish sects of Jesus' day—the Pharisees, Sadducees, Zealots, and Essenes all were guilty of exceptance. The Pharisees excepted anyone who was not faithful to the law and their traditions. The Sadducees, mostly conservative and from the wealthy aristocracy, excepted the sinful and poor. The Zealots viewed submission to Rome as an act of unfaithfulness to God and excepted anyone who disagreed. The Essenes excepted anyone who was not Essene.

Have you ever been excepted? It's not fun.

Why do we except people?

We except people when we allow ourselves to become isolated from them for any reason. When we isolate ourselves from sinners, we lose the ability to connect with them on any level. I have to work really hard to build relationships with non-Christians—which I do—because I know that the more I'm isolated from non-Christians, the less effective I'll be in sharing Jesus with them.

Luke wrote, "The Pharisees and the teachers of the law who belonged to their sect complained to his disciples" (Luke 5:30). Sects love fences because sects thrive on isolation. These Pharisees and teachers of the law were isolated from other religious groups, their fellow Jews, and the very people they were supposed to be helping. Their isolation rendered them ineffective as mediators between the weak and God, the one true source of all strength. And the Pharisees and teachers of the law prided themselves in their superiority to those people from whom they were isolated!

The more I'm isolated from non-Christians, the less effective I'll be in sharing Jesus with them.

This was no more evident than at opportunities of table fellowship. In his book *Contagious Holiness*, Craig Blomberg wrote, "Judaism viewed mealtimes as important occasions for drawing boundaries. Dining created an intimate setting in which one nurtured friendship with the right kind of people, eating the right kind of food."[5] Jesus ate the right kind of food with the wrong kind of people. Jesus refused to isolate himself from the very people he came to seek and to save.

Saving someone who is separated from you by a barrier is impossible.

I heard about a gardener who took great pride in caring for his lawn, which one year grew full of dandelions.

He tried every method and product to get rid of them, but nothing worked. Exasperated, he wrote the Department of Agriculture, explaining all he had done.

"What shall I try next?" he wrote.

"Try getting used to them," came the reply.

You may not like being around certain people, but I suggest you try getting used to them. Isolation is not an option for any true Christ follower.

In his Sermon on the Mount, Jesus taught, "You are the salt of the earth. . . . You are the light of the world" (Matthew 5:13-14). Salt and light affect their environments in significant ways. They both exist to make an impact. Salt in a saltshaker is worthless. Its value comes when it is poured out of the saltshaker. An oil lamp shining in bright daylight is not effective. Light and salt both make their biggest impact when they are not isolated from their environment.

The same is true of us, so let's fight any desire to practice exceptance.

"EXPARTEANCE"

Another barrier to true intimacy is just as troublesome: exparteance. Never heard of exparteance? Well, that's because I made up this word too.

Exparteance is a word I concocted from *ex parte*, a term used to describe a judicial proceeding conducted for the benefit of only one party—and it's not legal or fair. The Fifth Amendment of the US Constitution requires that all parties in a legal case receive due process. *Exparteance* is a word that

"You're Not Saying That?"

While in the Far East, my grown daughter and I got into a discussion with a Buddhist couple and their grown daughter who have been our friends for years. As we sat around their dinner table, the couple turned the conversation to spiritual things as they spoke of how much affection they had for our family . . . and something about our being "dedicated to our religion." My daughter and I sensed the conversation was heading to an important place, so we tried to tread cautiously as we began to talk about our beliefs.

Suddenly their daughter turned to me and said, "But you mean for you. A religion that's right for you. You're not saying that there's one true religion and that we should all believe that, are you? You're not saying that?"

Gulp. As gently as I could, I explained that some people believe that all religions are the same and they can choose one that appeals to them, but that for me, I would try to choose a right path. I wouldn't deliberately choose something I thought could be a wrong path.

I also was silently praying for the Lord to help me, because I really didn't know what to say. I wanted to be truthful without creating a barrier or a rift in the friendship.

As I spoke, they nodded agreeably, and we continued the discussion. The evening ended very warmly. They even laughed about how you're not supposed to discuss politics and religion with your friends. My daughter and I thanked them for being such good friends that we could comfortably discuss those things together (though, I confess, I hadn't felt completely comfortable during that part of the evening). I anticipate an unending and true friendship with them, and I'm praying for the Lord to bring others into their lives who also can help lead them to him.

—DARLENE—

describes what the Pharisees and teachers of the law were doing by looking out for their own interests and no one else's—including God's. It's an attempt to act only in your own best interest.

The Pharisees and teachers of the law revealed—in their dealings with people like Levi and other sinners—that everything they did was not for the benefit of others but for their own benefit. Only those within—and respectful of—the barriers around their group were to receive any of God's benefits.

This point of view reveals that these Jewish leaders were ignoring God's Word regarding the impact the Messiah would have when he brought about the year of the Lord's favor as described by the prophet Isaiah: "The Spirit of the Sovereign LORD is on me, because the LORD has anointed me to proclaim good news to the poor. He has sent me to bind up the brokenhearted, to proclaim freedom for the captives and release from darkness for the prisoners, to proclaim the year of the LORD's favor" (Isaiah 61:1-2). And as the Jewish leaders looked out for their own interests, they also revealed that they were ignoring Jesus' purpose, which he clearly claimed was a fulfillment of Isaiah's prophecy (Luke 4:16-21).

For those with ears to hear, Jesus' mission was clear: He came for the benefit of all people.

Exparteance is not just an ancient problem of old Jewish dudes; it's a huge problem today and a hindrance to evangelism.

We practice exparteance when our first question is "What about my needs?" instead of "What can I do to meet your needs?"

We practice exparteance when we expect others to conform to our standards of holiness.

We practice exparteance when we care more about being understood than we seek to understand.

We practice exparteance when we expect lost people to conform to our image of holiness instead of conforming to Christ's example of holiness.

We practice exparteance when we care more about winning an argument than winning someone for Jesus.

We practice exparteance when we expect the pastor to take care of the ninety-nine found sheep to the exception of the one lost sheep.

We practice exparteance when we expect lost people to "come worship with us" but never expect saved people to go and eat with sinners.

I was practicing exparteance, and Delmar Schroeder showed me a better way.

For many years Delmar Schroeder, who I mentioned in chapter 1, conducted a Bible study at a local bar on Saturday mornings. This Bible study was effective at reaching a lot of lost people for Jesus because—interesting fact—a lot of lost people hang out in bars. Well, now, because of Delmar's example, I do, too.

One of the people who came to Christ through Delmar's Bible study was an old-timer named Bert Dewey. Bert was a salty character. He'd lived a rough life full of women, drugs, and just all-around hard living. Bert was a committed member of The Fort Bible study. One Saturday, a group of rowdy bikers came into the bar and started getting loud and rambunctious. The Bible study wasn't quite done, so Bert Dewey—who wasn't saved at the time—stood up and asked, "Can you guys hold it down? We're a churchgoing bar."

I love that! "We're a churchgoing bar."

I love being a part of a bar-going church.

For the first couple of years, Bert attended that Bible study, but he wouldn't come to church. Well, one Sunday, as he was facing hip surgery, Bert came to Journey. He showed up late, sat uncomfortably on the back row, and left early, but I took notice and made sure to visit him at the hospital the next day.

Side note: Do you know that it's hard for lost people to ignore you when they are in a hospital bed? Just sayin'.

So Bert and I spoke for a couple of hours. He told me about his life and exploits, and I told him about Jesus. At one point he said, "Pastor, I was at church yesterday."

"Yes, I noticed," I replied.

"I don't usually go to church," he continued. He really meant, "I never go to church."

What Bert said next is one of the best compliments I've ever received: "Pastor, your church—that's some good sh—!"

I love that! I love being a part of a church that shares the love of Jesus in such a way that lost people also believe it's good . . . stuff!

I'm so grateful that Delmar took Jesus—and me—to that bar, because if it were up to me, I'd never ever, ever go to a bar. Up until Delmar led me out of my comfort zone, I'd never been to a bar, and bars were way out of my comfort zone. But now (even though I'm not a big drinker), because I'm no longer regularly practicing exparteance, I regularly experience the benefits of building new and dynamic relationships with people with whom I normally wouldn't associate. People like Bert Dewey, Delmar's friend, who became my friend, who then gave his life to Jesus and became Christ's friend.

I know on this issue I'm preaching to the choir. You picked up this book, so you get it. You obviously have a passion to reach people for Jesus. You live for the interests of others. I know that you hate exparteance too, and that gives me such hope.

The Pharisees and teachers of the law didn't get it, so they were limiting how they could be used by God to love people in his name. And we will too, unless we remain devoted to God's truth and his gospel of grace. I can't say it any better than Brennan Manning:

> Here is revelation bright as the evening star:
> Jesus comes for sinners, for those as outcast as
> tax collectors and for those caught up in squalid
> choices and failed dreams. He comes for corporate
> executives, street people, superstars, farmers,
> hookers, addicts, IRS agents, AIDS victims, and
> even used-car salesmen. Jesus not only talks with
> these people but also dines with them—fully aware
> that his table fellowship with sinners will raise the
> eyebrows of religious bureaucrats who hold up
> the robes and insignia of their authority to justify
> their condemnation of the truth and their rejection
> of the gospel of grace.[6]

Exparteance—devotion to our points of view and personal comfort—can hinder our efforts to reach lost people and help them get back to where they are supposed to be.

"EXTIRPATIENCE"

Another barrier to true intimacy is extirpatience. Never heard of extirpatience? That's because—as you now know—I like to make up words. *Extirpatience* is a noun that I made up from the verb *extirpate*, which means "to destroy completely."[7]

It seems that the Pharisees and teachers of the law were either unaware of or apathetic toward the impact their actions (or, more accurately, inactions) could have on the lives of lost people. Their social rejection of lost people was destructive to both the Pharisees' witness on behalf of God and to the potential for lost people to find the love of God through that witness. They didn't seem to care about lost people at all.

Not so with Jesus. Jesus cared about lost people. These Jewish leaders didn't care that Levi and his tax-collector friends were lost and spiritually sick, so they did nothing to help them. Jesus was committed to doing everything he could to help them. Jesus said, "It is not the healthy who need a doctor, but the sick. I have not come to call the righteous, but sinners to repentance" (Luke 5:31-32).

Doctors exist to help people, not destroy them. They don't have to persuade themselves to help people; it's who they are and what they do.

I witnessed this firsthand on a medical mission trip to Guatemala. Our team consisted of nurses, a few volunteers, and four doctors. We ran an eye clinic at a hospital and mobile medical clinics in local villages. I was amazed by the passion and energy the doctors showed as they interacted with sick people. As I watched them work, I felt like I was watching Jesus work.

One day my team saw about forty patients in sweltering conditions. Dr. Chris, a family physician from Greeley, saw a sad, listless little boy named Pedro toward the end of the day. Pedro moved very slowly, and we couldn't get him to smile. His mother said that he never played with his friends.

Dr. Chris quickly diagnosed the boy with a severe case of asthma. Pedro was using only about one-third of one lung to breathe. He had learned to control his movements and emotions to save his air. Dr. Chris determined that the boy's life was in danger and began treating him immediately. And the treatment worked. The transformation was amazing! Within twenty minutes Pedro was smiling and starting to play.

We all couldn't stop praising God for giving Dr. Chris a chance to change—and save—this little boy's life.

Dr. Chris walks this earth to save sick people's lives. Jesus walked this earth to save sick people's lives too, so he doesn't practice extirpatience; he heals and saves them instead.

May I take you back to The Fort Bar for a moment?

A few years ago, our church spent sixteen weeks studying the first edition of this book and learning what it means to truly love people as Jesus loved people. During that study, we hosted an event in our building on a Saturday night—a huge event for kids so their parents could take their non-Christian friends out for dinner to get to know them better.

The day before this event I called my wife to see which of our neighbors she thought we should take out to dinner, to which she responded, "We can't go out to eat because I'm volunteering at church for the kids' event on Saturday night."

I responded, "I can't ask the entire church to go out to eat with their neighbors and not do the same thing myself!"

She responded, "Why don't you go to The Fort on Saturday night?"

Wait, what?

Up to that point, I'd only been to The Fort Bar during the day because, as you know, the real "sinners" go to bars at night and I wasn't *that* committed to eating or drinking with sinners!

"Great idea!" I told Rhonda, after giving it some genuine consideration.

When I walked in the bar that Saturday night, Deanna— my friend and the bar owner—welcomed me to my regular seat at the end of the bar. She fixed me my regular drink, Mountain Dew, and my regular food order, a breakfast burrito.

Sitting next to me were two men, Richie and Louie. These two guys were regulars at The Fort and went out of their way to welcome me and make me feel comfortable. Over the next few hours the three of us spoke about life, politics, and the challenges of raising teenagers. As I was preparing to settle my bill and leave, Louie asked me an important question. "Hey, are you a pastor?"

Deanna and I had an agreement: She didn't tell people I was her pastor (yes, she comes to Journey, too) because that's a sure way to shut down most conversations with bar patrons.

"Yes, I am. How did you know?" I replied.

"Who else comes to a bar on Saturday night, drinks Mountain Dew, and eats a breakfast burrito?" he said. But then he continued, "You know Pastor Arron, Joel Osteen would never hang out with guys like us."

I don't think that's true or fair to Joel Osteen, but I understand what he was trying to say. He was trying to say, "Thank you for not treating us with exceptance, exparteance, or extirpatience." And also, I'm sure, "Thank you for inventing some very clever words."

Louie was really just trying to say, "Thanks for showing us what Christlike intimacy looks like."

FINDING INTIMACY
WITH NON-CHRISTIANS

- Join a club in your community that will put you in the position to build relationships with people who are not Christians.

- Invite your non-Christian neighbors to your home for dinner so that you can build a relationship with them.

- Identify something practical you can do to show the love of Christ for one of your neighbors, coworkers, or acquaintances. Take that first step in building a relationship with that person.

6
TOLERANCE

When the Pharisee who had invited him saw this,
he said to himself, "If this man were a prophet,
he would know who is touching him and what
kind of woman she is—that she is a sinner."

LUKE 7:39

Two things you never want to do. Never scream "Fire!" in a crowded theater, and never whisper the word *tolerance* in church, unless you want to be tied to a stake and burned. Okay, I'm being facetious and a little unfair, but some Christians don't seem to want anything to do with anything to do with *anything* that has the word *tolerance* in it.

We Christians love God and want to stand up for—and stand on—his Word, so we refuse to ignore, compromise on, or water down any of the clear teachings of Scripture about sinful lifestyles, wrong beliefs, sexually deviant behavior, socialism, secular humanism, Muzak, and domesticated cats. And this is good because none of these things should be tolerated, but in this chapter I'm not encouraging anyone to be tolerant of sinful lifestyles, beliefs, or things; I'm talking about being tolerant of sinful people.

Tolerance is allowing someone, or something, to be.

INTOLERANT OF SIN

Continued unrepentant sin should never be tolerated in the person of any Christian. As Paul wrote to the Christians in Rome, "What shall we say, then? Shall we go on sinning so that grace may increase? By no means! We are those who have died to sin; how can we live in it any longer?" (Romans 6:1-2).

Despite what my five-year-old daughter Payton thought, we are all sinners (Romans 3:23). In home school a few years ago, my wife was sitting on the couch with our two young boys, teaching a lesson about sin. My youngest son, Sylas, asked, "Mommy, what is sin?" so Rhonda explained to him that sin is when we disobey God. She then went on to explain to the boys that we are all sinners. Payton was in the kitchen getting a drink of water—and not a part of the lesson—but when she heard this, she announced with a look of horror on her face, "I'm not a sinner!"

Rhonda replied, "Well, sweetie, you actually are—we all are."

"But I'm not a sinner!" Payton exclaimed again.

Always the wise teacher, Rhonda said, "Well, sweetie, you're actually sinning a little bit right now."

Continued unrepentant sin should never be tolerated in the body of Christ. Sin in the church is like a cancer that, if left untreated, leads to death. We are supposed to eat with non-Christian sinners but not with unrepentant Christian ones. The

Sin in the church is like a cancer that, if left untreated, leads to death.

apostle Paul wrote to Christians who were tolerating an incestuous relationship within their congregation: "I wrote to you in my letter not to associate with sexually immoral people—not at all meaning the people of this world who are immoral, or the greedy and swindlers, or idolaters. In that case you would have to leave this world. But now I am writing to you that you must not associate with anyone who claims to be a brother or sister but is sexually immoral or greedy, an idolater or slanderer, a drunkard or swindler. Do not even eat with such people" (1 Corinthians 5:9-11).

Sinners should always be allowed in our presence. It's their only hope. It's our only hope for reaching them.

But we are commanded not to eat with another Christian who is tolerating sexual immorality, greed, idolatry, slander, drunkenness, or swindling in his or her life.

TOLERANT OF SINNERS

Sinners should always be tolerated.

Jesus made this point when he allowed a sinful woman to be in his presence—allowed her to wipe his feet with her hair, kiss his feet, and pour perfume on his feet while he ate at Simon the Pharisee's house (Luke 7:36-50).

This confused Simon. He didn't understand why a man of Jesus' stature would tolerate this woman. Luke doesn't tell us the nature of her sin, but from Luke's comment that she was "a woman in that town who lived a sinful life" (Luke 7:37), we infer that she most likely was a prostitute. Simon was befuddled. If Jesus really was a prophet of God—as the people claimed— why would he allow a woman like this to be in his presence?

Why would Jesus allow himself to be contaminated by the proceeds of that woman's evil work? Wasn't he condoning her lifestyle by receiving her attention and allowing her to anoint his feet with the spoils of her evil trade?

Of course not!

He wasn't condoning her actions. He was just loving her.

Jesus was more tolerant of lost people than we will ever be, because he loved lost people more than we ever will. Tolerance is viewed by many in the church as watering down the message of Jesus, but when we look at how Jesus interacted with sinners who were in need of salvation, we learn that tolerance toward sinners was key to how he reached out to them. He chose to be with sinners because he wanted them to have hope. He allowed this prostitute to be in his presence at this dinner because he wanted her to be with him at the banquet he will host in eternity.

Truth cannot be sacrificed at the altar of pretended tolerance. Real tolerance is deference to all ideas, not indifference to the truth.
—RAVI ZACHARIAS

It's all about the choices we make, and sometimes we make bad choices. Sin is about choice. We choose to sin.

Faith is also about choice. We choose to believe.

This woman had made some bad choices in the past, but those

choices hadn't made her intolerable, just sinful, so Jesus chose to have faith in the power of love lived out in her presence.

Tolerance is really an act of faith.

When it comes to sharing our faith in Jesus, allowing someone to be in our presence is a statement of our faith that coexistence between Christians and non-Christians will result in positive changes.

WE MUST HAVE FAITH IN PEOPLE

We must believe that people can change.

Unlike many of the people in Contessa's world, my friend Keith didn't write Contessa off as a lost cause, because he believed she could change.

When he first met Contessa, she was almost completely incapable of expressing herself verbally, so she wrote notes to him and slid the notes across the table. She had been hurt deeply by life and some really bad people. She was wounded and needed someone to believe that she could be rescued from the darkness enveloping her life.

Keith believes in God, so he believed that—with God's help and through the power of the Holy Spirit—Contessa could be changed.

He and many other Christians ate with Contessa at a common meal every Saturday before the Celebrate Recovery meeting. Keith and the other Christians involved in Celebrate Recovery refused to be shocked by anything Contessa shared with them, and they refused to stop believing in her. The people she encountered at church—including me—just loved her, encouraged her, and tolerated her while constantly speaking hope and truth into her life. I had the blessing of leading a ministry in which Contessa was involved, and I got to know her very well. And after more than a year, because of the love of a bunch of good people who believed that she could change, Contessa gave her life to Jesus Christ.

Contessa, a girl who once struggled to verbalize even the simplest thought with a stranger, now shares her testimony with Celebrate Recovery groups around her hometown. She's an amazing person who was changed by God and the faith of some wonderful Christians. Praise God!

We are all sinners who sin. We are not sin. There's a difference.

Simon the Pharisee had no faith in the woman who knelt at Jesus' feet. He didn't believe she could ever change, even though the evidence of her transformation was dripping from Jesus' feet onto the floor, running down her face, moistening her hair, and filling his home with its sweet fragrance. He wondered why Jesus couldn't see "what kind of woman she [was]" (Luke 7:39), because that was all he could see. She was not sin, but only Jesus could see that.

By the way, let me pause here and point out something that can hinder our efforts to share our faith with non-Christians. Please remember that, through Jesus, you and I are not our worst sin.

Do you know that?

When you look in the mirror, what do you see? Do you have a hard time seeing past the bad choice you made on prom night your junior year of high school? Do you have a hard time seeing past the three guys you slept with in college? Do you have a hard time seeing past the deceptive and manipulative games you played to get that promotion last year?

We are all sinners who sin. We are not sin. There's a difference. Sinners are to be loved; sin is not. We sometimes, despite what we say, seem to have a hard time separating the sin from the sinner. Who do we think we are, showing no grace to those who need it most?

Who died and made us sinners God? No one!

Who died to make us sinners godly? God's Son did.

God loves sinners. That's the point of John 3:16: "For God so loved the world that he gave his one and only Son." And Paul wrote in Romans 5:8, "God demonstrates his own love for us in this: While we were still sinners, Christ died for us."

God's love, demonstrated, looks like Jesus dying on a cross for sinners, while they're still sinners.

God doesn't hate sinners; he loves them. He loves you. He loves me.

He loves drug dealers, child abusers, tax cheats, crossdressers, women chasers, men chasers, liars, drunkards, swindlers, dirty politicians, movie stars who bash Christianity, telemarketers, and prostitutes with alabaster jars of perfume. He tolerates them—he allows them to be—because he has faith that everyone can change if given the chance.

Which is exactly what Kris Hogan believes too.

Kris Hogan is the head football coach at Grapevine Faith Christian School in Grapevine, Texas. His faith in the ability of his team and the fans at his school to make good choices transformed a football field in Grapevine into a sanctuary, football fans into saints, and sinners into believers.

The football game between Gainesville State School and Grapevine Faith Christian School in November 2008 would have been an ordinary football game between two Texas high schools if Hogan hadn't decided to show Christlike tolerance to the players from Gainesville State.

What kind of situation would require Coach Hogan to show tolerance to a bunch of high school football players? Are they cheaters? Thieves? Druggies? Gangbangers? Are they "sinners"?

Make it an object of constant study, and of daily reflection and prayer, to learn how to deal with sinners so as to promote their conversion.
—CHARLES G. FINNEY, *LECTURES ON REVIVALS OF RELIGION*

Well, some of them are a few of these and—like the rest of us—all are the latter. Gainesville State School is a maximum-security correctional facility seventy-five miles north of Dallas. Every player on Gainesville State's roster has been convicted of something, and every game for them is a road game. The fourteen Gainesville players arrive at every game escorted not by cheerleaders and doting parents wearing jerseys, but by twelve uniformed officers.

No one comes to their games.

No one cheers for them.

No one seems to believe in them—at least, that's what they believed until that special November night.

Coach Hogan decided to do something special for the Gainesville players. Before his team's game with Gainesville State, he sent an e-mail to his players and the fans of the

Faithful (good name, huh?) with the following directive: "Here's the message I want you to send: You are just as valuable as any other person on planet Earth."[1]

Some people were confused at first. "Why are we doing this?" To which Coach Hogan replied, "Imagine if you didn't have a home life. Imagine if everybody had pretty much given up on you. Now imagine what it would mean for hundreds of people to suddenly believe in you."[2]

Imagine what would happen if every Christian suddenly believed in every sinner.

The Grapevine Faithful responded in amazing fashion.

Before the game they took the field and made a forty-yard spirit line with a banner for the Gainesville Tornadoes to run through. More than two hundred Faith fans sat on the Gainesville side of the field to cheer the Gainesville players on—by name. Half of Faith's cheerleaders stood behind the Tornadoes and cheered them on for the entire game.

The Gainesville Tornadoes were so overwhelmed that, although they lost the game (and maintained their perfect 0–9 schedule for the season), at the end of the game they reacted as if they'd just won the Super Bowl—jumping up and down and giving their coach a Gatorade bath.

After the game both teams gathered in the middle of the field for prayer, and Gainesville's quarterback and middle linebacker surprised everyone by volunteering to pray. Isaiah (only first names are released by the prison) prayed, "Lord, I don't know how this happened, so I don't know how to say thank You, but I never would've known there was so many people in the world that cared about us."[3]

Imagine what would happen if every Christian suddenly believed in every sinner.

When the game was over and the Gainesville players boarded the bus, each player was handed a bag for the ride home—with a burger, fries, can of soda, some candy, a Bible, and a encouraging letter from a Faith player.

A little tolerance—a little faith that people should be allowed to be accepted in our presence so they can be given a chance to change—can give all sinners a reason to believe.

WE MUST HAVE FAITH IN GOD

Do you believe that all sinners have a reason to believe?

Do you believe that God can forgive anyone of anything?

Do you really?

Jeffrey Dahmer, while in prison for murdering, dismembering, and cannibalizing his victims, gave his life to Jesus Christ and was baptized for the forgiveness of sins.[4] Does this news make you happy, or do you share the sentiments of the college professor who said, "If Dahmer's in heaven, I don't want to be there"?[5]

I have faith that with Jesus there are no lost causes. The woman at Simon the Pharisee's house had been written off by the "faithful" people around her. Simon had already judged her and ruled that she was a sinner, untouchable, intolerable. She was not to be allowed in the presence of any self-respecting prophet.

Jesus disagreed. He judged her a sinner and forgave her of her sins (Luke 7:47-48).

She Didn't Judge Me

I was around forty years old. For many of those years, I had a hole in my soul that I kept trying to fill with all the wrong things: alcohol, bad relationships, etc. Finally, a coworker suggested a support group. *What can it hurt?* I thought.

The group met weekly. There I met Betty. I don't know why we gravitated toward each other, but we did. After the meetings, the group would go to a local restaurant to eat. We would all try to squeeze into a big booth, and Betty and I always tried to sit together. I didn't know then that when Betty and I were eating together, we were doing something called fellowship.

Betty didn't share her faith in Jesus with me overtly, but there was something about her. . . . We weren't likely friends. I cursed like a truck driver. She never did, yet she didn't judge me for doing it. I smoked and drank. She never did, yet she didn't judge me for doing those things either. We exchanged phone numbers and soon were friends outside of the group.

One day she asked if I would like to go to church with her. *What can it hurt?* I thought. Not long after that, I was baptized. On that day I told the Lord I couldn't give up smoking and drinking, so he would have to do it for me. He did.

Well, now I'm sixty years old. My dear friend has moved away, but when we get together it's as though we have never been apart. I thank God daily for my dear friend Betty, and that she never gave up on me.

—SUE—

Now, we say that we believe God can do anything, but usually that's in the context of healing cancer, restoring broken marriages, keeping us out of bankruptcy, and allowing the Indians to win the World Series (go Cubs!). Do we really believe that all lost people can have the hope of forgiveness—that God can forgive anyone of anything? If so, then that will change everything.

We will tolerate sinners—allowing them in our presence—because we believe that God has the power for positive change.

We will tolerate sinners because we believe that with God there are no lost causes.

Do we really believe that all lost people can have the hope of forgiveness—that God can forgive anyone of anything?

We'll make a spirit tunnel for sinners, cheering as they break through the banner. We'll cheer for them while they play, and we'll celebrate as the sinners we tolerated dump Gatorade on their coach's head out of gratitude for the forgiveness that can only be found through God.

I believe it can happen.

It happened at Simon the Pharisee's house.

It happened on a football field in Grapevine, Texas. It can happen while you're eating with a sinner.

Remember how this chapter started with two things you never want to do? Let's rewrite the second one: Never be intolerant of sinners. So say it—no, scream it—in your workplace, your neighborhood, your home, your church, and at the local football field if you must.

"Tolerance!"

PRACTICING CHRISTLIKE TOLERANCE

- Write down the name of someone you have a hard time tolerating.

- Based on what you know about God, list three good things that God has done to show his love for that person.

- List one thing you can do today to show your love for that person.

- Start praying for the person—by name—right now.

7

RESOLVE

As the time approached for him to be taken up to heaven,
Jesus resolutely set out for Jerusalem.

LUKE 9:51

There are a lot of famous quitters out there.

Richard Nixon, the thirty-seventh president of the United States, was a quitter twice over. When he lost the presidential election in 1960 and his run to be governor in 1962, Richard Nixon announced that he was through with politics. Which was true until he was elected president twice, only to be forced to leave the office in 1974.

In 1952, Florence Chadwick attempted to become the first woman to swim from Catalina Island to the California coastline. During her swim she was surrounded by a fleet of small boats prepared to protect her from sharks and rescue her if she got hurt or grew tired. Gradually a thick bank of

How few there are who have courage enough to own their Faults, or resolution enough to mend them!

—BENJAMIN FRANKLIN, *POOR RICHARD'S ALMANAC, 1743*

fog settled on the water. Florence was well trained, but the fog disoriented her and made her doubt her ability to reach the coast. After nearly sixteen hours, Florence quit swimming and asked to be pulled out of the water. As she sat in the boat, Florence's disappointment grew when she realized she had stopped swimming just one mile from her destination.

Yes, there are a lot of famous quitters out there, but there are also a lot of famous nonquitters out there. Take . . . Florence Chadwick, for example. Yes, the same Florence Chadwick.

Florence had been inspired to start distance swimming when she read about the exploits of Gertrude Ederle, the first woman ever to swim the twenty-three miles across the English Channel. Florence wanted to surpass Ederle's record and become the first woman to swim the English Channel both ways—from France to England as well as from England to France. She took a job working for the Arabian-American Oil Company, moved to Saudi Arabia with the company, and began training in the rough waters of the Persian Gulf. She was so dedicated to her goal that she swam before and after work and trained for up to ten hours a day on her days off.

In 1950, Florence quit her job and went to France. She filled out an application in a local newspaper to find sponsors for her swim across the Channel, but since she was unknown, her application was rejected. Undeterred, in August 1950, after training for two years, Florence decided to swim the

English Channel anyway, and she ended up breaking the world record set twenty-four years earlier by Gertrude Ederle.

Two years after that record-setting swim, as you now know, Florence attempted to swim between Catalina Island and the California coast and quit only a mile short of her goal. When a reporter asked why she had quit, Florence said, "Look, I'm not excusing myself, but if I could have seen land I know I could have made it." When the fog moved in, her hope moved out.

Two months later, Florence tried again. During this second swim between Catalina and the coast, the same thick fog set in, but this time, with intense resolve, Florence made it to the coast by keeping an image of the shoreline in her mind while she swam.[1]

And that teaches us the first key to keeping our resolve as we seek to reach people for Jesus: having a clear goal.

WE MUST HAVE A CLEAR GOAL

We learn the importance of having a clear goal from another famous nonquitter: Jesus.

Jesus had a clear goal in mind as he headed for Jerusalem. His goal was twofold: to die for the sins of humankind and then to go to heaven to prepare a place for all who put their faith in him. With this clear goal in mind, Jesus "resolutely set out for Jerusalem" (Luke 9:51). A more literal translation of the Greek words used in this verse is "Jesus set his face to go to Jerusalem."

Jesus set his face to go to Jerusalem, knowing that in

Jerusalem he would die. He had a clear goal, and he was resolved to reach it—no matter what.

What is your face set on? Losing twenty pounds? Exercising every day? Starting piano lessons? Getting out of debt? Working more? Working less? Reading a book? Fixing your relationship with your spouse? Fixing your relationship with God? These are all good goals and worthy of achieving.

Florence Chadwick's face was set on the California coast.

My face is set on going to heaven and taking as many people with me as possible.

Jesus' face was set on a cross on a hill at the edge of town, and nothing was going to deter him from fulfilling his mission. Nothing will stop us from reaching lost people if we are as resolved as Jesus to reach them.

Nothing will stop us from reaching lost people if we are as resolved as Jesus to reach them.

Goals are easier set than done. Ask Thomas Edison.

Thomas Edison's face was set on the light bulb. (This is a metaphor, painful, and should never be tried at home!) When Edison first attended school, his teachers complained that he was too slow. This remedial student went on to produce more than 1,300 inventions. In the process of inventing the light bulb, Edison tried more than two thousand experiments. When a young reporter asked him how it felt to fail so many times, Edison reportedly said, "I never failed once. I invented the light bulb. It just happened to be a two-thousand step process." Edison had a clear goal and resolved early on to do whatever it took to reach that goal. No whining. No complaining. No quitting.

I hope you make it your goal to reach as many people as you can for Jesus—to eat with as many sinners as possible— but I also want you to understand that it's going to take resolve on your part to reach this goal.

I hope you make it your goal to reach as many people as you can for Jesus—to eat with as many sinners as possible.

You are going to face obstacles on your way to your Jerusalem.

Yes, I did say "your Jerusalem." You have a Jerusalem. Maybe more than one. We all do— a place, or places, God plans for us to go, our destiny, a place of extraordinary service and sacrifice, a higher purpose for which we were placed on this planet.

Your Jerusalem may be across the street or across the Pacific Ocean.

Your Jerusalem may be your most annoying neighbor, the one you think poisoned your dog.

Your Jerusalem may be a family reunion.

Your Jerusalem may work three cubicles away.

Your Jerusalem may be receiving the divorce papers you served him with today.

Your Jerusalem may be a place of indescribable joy, or it may be a place of unbelievable suffering.

Jerusalem meant death for Jesus, yet he was resolved to get there because it meant life for us. What are you resolved to do?

John Milton was resolved to write *Paradise Lost*, so he did—several years after losing his eyesight at the age of forty-four.

German composer Ludwig van Beethoven was resolved

to compose great music, so he did, even after he began to lose his hearing in his twenties. He wrote some of his greatest music, including a number of symphonies, after going completely deaf.

Wilma Rudolph was born prematurely. As a child she battled pneumonia, scarlet fever, and polio. Even though she wore leg braces at times, she was resolved to run, so she did— going on to win three Olympic gold medals.

Judy, one of my Sunday school teachers and neighbors when I was in elementary school, resolved to reach her husband for Christ, so she asked us to pray for him every Sunday. She had a clear goal in mind: her husband with her for all eternity. He was a good man but not a Christ follower, and she longed for him to share more than just this life with her. Nothing could deter her confidence that Neal would one day give his life to Christ, so we all prayed. Week after week and year after year, we prayed for her husband to come to Christ. And one day he did. I had the pleasure of serving with him in my first paid ministry. I praise God for "Miss Judy's" resolve.

I'm resolved to reach lost people for Jesus too. I'm obsessed with it. I'm consumed with it, and I want you to be consumed with it too, so that you'll resolve to consume as much food with sinners as possible.

We can't let pride keep us from eating with sinners. We can't let religious piety keep us from eating with sinners. We can't let comfort keep us from eating with sinners. We can't let busyness keep us from eating with sinners.

We must not let anything keep us from eating with sinners! Set your face on your Jerusalem and don't let misguided

David's Story

David's weekly routine was to drop off his girls at church early on Sunday mornings—and then sit in the parking lot until the service was over. Every so often I would stick my head out the church doors and see him sitting there with his books, notebook, and pen. Seeing his silhouette in the car prompted me to exercise my pastoral duty, walk over, and invite him into the service. Each week the same answer: "No thanks, but thank you for inviting me." More than a year went by before David took me up on an invitation. But this invitation was different.

David's daughter, Kristy, who was hearing impaired, was performing in a group song accompanied by signing. So David joined us for church that Sunday. It just happened that after the service, we were going to have a dinner. Right after the service, I invited him to stay and eat with us. He said okay, and I about hit the floor.

I couldn't help but think that all those invitations to come inside had built a relationship between David and me. I felt a connection while we sat at that first meal together, talking about his work and his life. I also thought that this was perhaps the beginning of something more with David. I was right.

David and I began doing lunch together over the next few months. He came prepared each time with a list of questions about God, the Bible, Jesus, and the Christian life. I saw his trust in the idea of church and his faith in the person of Christ move to a better place. And then one day over chicken strips and potato wedges, David declared, "I believe that Jesus died for my sins, and I want to spend the rest of my life letting God know how grateful I am for his blessings." Praise God!

—TIM—

disciples keep you from following God's plan and fulfilling your destiny.

WE MUST HAVE A RELENTLESS DESIRE TO REACH OUR GOAL

Luke 9:51-56 tells us that Jesus sent messengers ahead to a village in Samaria to arrange for lodging, but the people there did not welcome Jesus, because he and his disciples were heading for Jerusalem. Samaritans and Jews had not gotten along for quite some time.

Facing Challenges from Outsiders

Jesus was in Galilee when he set out for the Feast of Tabernacles in Jerusalem (John 7:1-10). He would have to pass through Samaria to get to Jerusalem to the south. Samaritans resented their country being used as a highway to the Jewish feasts, so their opposition to Jesus' visit was not a surprise.

This obstacle didn't stop Jesus. He simply went to another village. Those first Samaritans didn't realize the blessings they missed by not receiving Jesus into their village.

As we work to reach lost people for Jesus, we're going to face challenges from people in the world who don't want us to succeed.

Facing Challenges from Insiders

We should expect challenges from outsiders, but we must not be surprised when we face challenges from insiders, because that will happen too.

Two of Jesus' disciples were ticked off at this Samaritan rejection. "Lord, do you want us to call fire down from heaven to destroy them?" they asked (Luke 9:54).

Call fire down from heaven?

I could have voted for calling down a long rainstorm, or hail, or dove poop, or even a deluge of Justin Bieber's greatest hits. Heaven knows that would have been a terrible fate, but even that would not have pleased the disciples. They wanted these Samaritans dead, but not just dead—they wanted these Samaritans to suffer. Were they not listening when Jesus said, "To you who are listening I say: Love your enemies, do good to those who hate you"? (Luke 6:27).

Jesus wanted these Samaritans—and all sinners—to live, not die, so he rebuked his disciples and set his face on Jerusalem, refusing to let anything keep him from what he had resolved to do.

PRESSING ON

There are a lot of famous quitters, but Jesus was not one of them.

Neither was Sir Edmund Hillary, who had climbed many mountains but was set on conquering Mount Everest.

His 1952 attempt failed, as had at least seven major missions before his. A few weeks later, while speaking in England, he walked to the edge of the stage and pointed to a picture of the mountain. He shouted, "Mount Everest, you beat me the first time, but I'll beat you the next time because you've grown all you are going to grow . . . but I'm still growing!"

Hillary didn't quit. Despite external and internal challenges, he pressed on, and on May 29, 1953, he became the first man to climb Mount Everest.

As you climb your Everest, you're going to be tempted to quit, but resolve now that you're never going to stop growing and you're not going to let anything deter your relentless pursuit.

Resolve to follow John Stephen Akhwari's example. He's my favorite nonquitter of all time, other than Jesus.

Akhwari had just finished the Olympic marathon. Early in the race he fell and injured his leg severely. Outsiders tried to deter him from finishing. Medical personnel urged him to drop out of the race so they could tend to his injuries, but he refused to quit. His face was set on the finish line.

Pain from within his body tried to deter him. Each step was excruciating, but Akhwari pressed on, resolved to finish the race.

And late in the evening, an hour after the marathon had been declared over, out of the cold darkness he came. Akhwari of Tanzania entered at the far end of the Olympic stadium in Mexico City, pain hobbling his every step, his leg bloody and bandaged. Only a few spectators remained. But Akhwari pressed on.

As he crossed the finish line, the spectators roared out their appreciation. They realized that they were witnesses to something truly special.

After the race, a reporter asked Akhwari why he had not retired from the race, since he had no chance of winning.

His answer: "My country did not send me 5,000 miles just to start the race. They sent me to finish the race." [2]

Akhwari's face was set on the finish line, so he refused to quit.

My face is set on reaching lost people for Jesus. It's why I'm here on this planet. It's why Jesus was sent to this earth.

I must finish my race. You must too. What is your face set on? Is it set on eating with sinners? If so, on to Jerusalem.

ASSESSING YOUR RESOLVE

- List three goals you have already accomplished.

- Beside each accomplished goal, list one life change you made that enabled you to reach that goal.

- What is your face set on right now?

8

URGENCY

The harvest is plentiful, but the workers are few.
Ask the Lord of the harvest, therefore, to send
out workers into his harvest field.

LUKE 10:2

He and his crew had to make a quick decision.

With more than forty years of flying experience, Captain Chesley B. Sullenberger III—known to his friends as Sully—was pretty sure that at least one of the birds that flew in front of US Airways Flight 1549 as it took off had been sucked into the engines of the plane.[1] When the plane started to shake and alarms sounded all over the cockpit, Sully knew that the flight was in serious trouble.

An air traffic controller at La Guardia Airport, where the plane took off, advised Sully to try to bring the plane in at nearby Teterboro airport in New Jersey, but Sully knew the plane would not make it that far. He decided to land the

If time be of all things the most
precious, wasting time must
be the greatest prodigality.
—BENJAMIN FRANKLIN,
THE WAY TO WEALTH

plane like a glider in the Hudson River.

The alarms in the cockpit weren't the only alarms sounding. Almost as soon as Sully's words "double bird strike"[2] reached the air traffic controller's headset, alarms went off for first responders all over New York City. But as they mobilized, Sully flew down the Hudson River, clearing the George Washington Bridge by about nine hundred feet, and calmly landed his plane in the middle of the river.

At this point, alarms started sounding all over the country.

Officials at the Transportation Security Administration in northern Virginia were reviewing presidential inauguration plans when alarms interrupted their meeting. Immediately, everyone in the room sprang into action. "If there is a plane that is behaving erratically in New York City, everyone moves," one official said.[3]

Alarms sounded as far away as the North American Aerospace Defense Command (NORAD) in Colorado Springs. As the news of an aircraft emergency in the La Guardia area came over the speakers in the ceilings and on desks at NORAD, "a hush fell over the 30 or so people in the room."[4] Everyone recognized that 155 lives—and possibly more, if this were a terrorist attack—were in danger.

Alarms are important and necessary, but we don't always appreciate that, do we?

Most of us begin our day with the sound of an alarm startling us out of a completely snug and relaxed state. But if we stop to think about it—and focus on the results—alarms are actually quite positive calls to action.

The sounding of an oven alarm means the cookies are done.

The sounding of a fire alarm means there is a fire in the building and you now have a chance to get out.

The sounding of an alarm clock means that a day full of opportunities has begun and it's time to get out of bed.

The sounding of my neighbor's car alarm means absolutely nothing!

God sounded an alarm to his people through the prophet Isaiah, saying, "Arise, shine, for your light has come, and the glory of the LORD rises upon you" (60:1). When Jesus' followers sleep, lost people are in jeopardy. God has plans for his church to be at rest (Hebrews 4:9-10; Revelation 14:13), but not on this side of heaven.

That's why—through Paul—God sounded the alarm to the Christians in Rome, saying, "The hour has already come for you to wake up from your slumber, because our salvation is nearer now than when we first believed" (Romans 13:11).

That's why—through John—God sounded the alarm to the church, saying, "Wake up! Strengthen what remains and is about to die. . . . But if you do not wake up, I will come like a thief, and you will not know at what time I will come to you" (Revelation 3:2-3).

You may not hear it, but the alarm is sounding:

On any given day, 42 percent of ten- to seventeen-year-olds are exposed to online porn.[5]

Thirty-three percent of sixteen-year-olds, 48 percent of all seventeen-year-olds, and 61 percent of eighteen-year-olds in the United States have had sex at least once.

Although fifteen- to twenty-four-year-olds represent only one quarter of the sexually active population, they account for nearly half (9.1 million) of the 18.9 million new cases of sexually transmitted infections each year.[6]

In 2014, more than fifteen hundred children in the United States died from child abuse and neglect. That is just over four fatalities every day.[7]

Each year about 55.3 million people die. Each day 151,600 people die. Each hour 6,316 people die. Each minute 105 people die.[8]

Can you hear it? The alarm is sounding.

One morning a young girl awoke, and as she was going downstairs to get something to eat, the grandfather clock struck seven o'clock. But it didn't stop there. It went right on striking—eight, nine, ten, eleven, twelve—and still it didn't stop—thirteen, fourteen, fifteen . . . The girl ran back upstairs, shouting to the whole family, "Get up! It's later than it ever was!"

I agree. It's later than it ever was! What are we waiting for? What's it going to take to get the church to wake up and get to work?

From what we read in Luke 10:2, the alarm is sounding for two reasons.

THE HARVEST IS READY

The first reason the alarm is sounding is that the harvest is ready.

I was born and raised in suburbia. I'd been on farms and around farmers often in my life and had even put up hay a time or two, but I had never been on a farm during the harvest until a few years ago. My friend Gary (the elder at my church who believed there are no lost causes) arranged for me to get a ride on a cutter used for harvesting corn. I learned how important it is to get the harvest brought in at just the right time. Too early and the corn won't be ready. Too late and it will be ruined.

I learned that everything the farmer does is to bring in a good harvest. He plants his fields and fertilizes so his crops will be ready at just the right time. With great urgency, he prepares his machinery for the harvest, hires extra help for the harvest, and arranges for delivery of his harvest. The farmer depends on a good harvest for his financial survival.

Just as it does for a farmer, the harvest means everything to Jesus.

With great urgency Jesus assembled a group of people to help him bring in the harvest. He'd already sent out the twelve disciples to start bringing in the harvest, but he had bigger plans, so he gathered seventy-two others and sent them out ahead of him, two by two, to every town and place where he was about to go. As he sent them out, he told them, "The harvest is plentiful" (Luke 10:2).

Can't you see it? The harvest.

It looks like a coworker who starts crying at lunch when you ask her about things at home.

It looks like an elderly neighbor who sits by himself on

his front porch in the chair next to the chair where his wife used to sit.

It looks like an angry boss who asks you why you go to a men's prayer group before work on Thursday morning.

It looks like your kid's teacher.

It looks like the guy in line at the 7-Eleven on Saturday night, waiting to spend fifty dollars on lottery tickets, hoping to finally have something that will change his miserable life.

It looks like the classmate you've reconnected with on Facebook.

It looks like the attractive woman with the low-cut top sitting next to you on the plane and trying to flirt as you discuss the weather.

It looks like the young couple at the end of the street who seem overwhelmed taking care of their three little kids.

It looks like your alcoholic father.

It looks like your teenage daughter who acts like she doesn't want you around only because she needs you so desperately.

It looks like the person you're going to eat with at McDonald's next Wednesday because you want to eat with him in heaven for all eternity.

It looked like Evan, a young man in the youth group of a church where I served as youth minister. When I met Evan for the first time, I was sure that he hated me, church, other young people, the music we were playing, and every word that came out of my mouth. His hair was long, his '80s rock-band T-shirt was ratty, and he looked a little scary. A relative

A Serving Server

I was married to a music minister in Bible college and working as a server at a well-known Chinese restaurant in central Florida. I loved being a server. I also loved being a Christian. At this time, I had been a Christian for only a few years, and I was pumped up. I wanted to do more, so I asked God to do more.

Every day before my shift, I would ask God to open the door to have one conversation with one person about his love, and if he chose to open the door twenty-five times, I would be ready. I made some really great friends at work. Some of these friendships grew while we folded napkins after our shift.

On one special night, I folded napkins with my friend Bill. He was over six feet tall, loved basketball, and was really nice, so I thought it would be cool to get to know him more. We talked about our shift, how much money we made, and then the door opened. Somehow we started talking about Jesus, baptism, salvation, and God's love.

He thought about our conversation, and a week later I had the privilege of baptizing Bill, another server named Tammy, and her friend Sophie. Bill started coming to church with us, eventually getting involved in leading the youth ministry at another church in town. He's now getting a master's degree in theology.

It was so amazing how God turned a Chinese restaurant into a place of worship. Only God could combine lo mein and love to grow his Kingdom!

—NICOLE—

had made him come to church, and he wasn't too excited about it—but we were excited to see him.

Every time I see a kid like Evan, I see an opportunity for a great harvest. I saw an opportunity with Evan. I also saw that we couldn't wait to reach out to Evan. Based on his behavior, I wasn't sure we'd ever see him again. Recognizing the urgency, another youth sponsor and I made a beeline to Evan, introduced ourselves, and helped to get him engaged in the activities of the night. We started sharing the unconditional love of Jesus with him.

By the end of the evening, Evan seemed to be enjoying himself. He came back the next week and the week after that.

I ate with Evan and the other youth regularly, but over the next few weeks I tuned in to Evan especially and worked hard at getting to know him and helping him get to know the Jesus who loved him. I came to know Evan as a really nice young man who'd experienced a lot of pain in his life. He wasn't hateful at all but loving and a little misunderstood. In Evan I could see a young man with the potential to do great things for God. The other youth sponsors and young people could see the potential harvest represented in Evan's life, too, and invested themselves heavily in building relationships with him.

Through his relationships with the other youth, the youth sponsors, and me, Evan began a relationship with Jesus Christ, allowed God to transform his life, and now is serving the Lord in the worship ministry of his church.

In high school, while visiting friends in Ohio, my brother and I were helping to put up hay in their barn when their father said something that changed the way I look at evangelism: "You have to make hay while the sun is shining."

The sun is shining. The harvest is ready. There are people like Evan everywhere. We must—with a sense of urgency—work to bring the harvest in.

The Mennonites have a saying: "We are living in the time of God's patience." God is patiently waiting for us to open our eyes, to notice that the harvest is ready, and to help him bring it in before it's too late.

THE WORKERS ARE FEW

As we look at the next part of Luke 10:2, we see that the alarm is sounding not just because the harvest is ready but also because Jesus wants more workers to join him in bringing it in. As he sent out the seventy-two workers, he said, "The harvest is plentiful, but the workers are few."

There's nothing worse for a farmer than to have the harvest ready but not have enough help to bring it in. Ask Norman Fleck.

Norman is a wheat farmer in South Dakota who was unable to bring in his harvest because he had suffered a spinal cord injury in an ATV accident and was partially paralyzed. Family and friends had been helping Norman and his family during the summer to prepare for the harvest, but Norman knew that he needed more help or he might lose his wheat crop. That's where Farm Rescue came in.

Farm Rescue is a nonprofit organization that plants and harvests crops, free of charge, for family farmers who need help because of a crisis. Norman knew that his situation was urgent, so from his hospital bed he contacted Farm Rescue representatives to see if they might be able to help bring in his wheat harvest. They eagerly agreed.

There's nothing worse for a farmer than to have the harvest ready but not have enough help to bring it in.

Farm Rescue came at just the right time and saved Norman's wheat harvest because the people sent by Farm Rescue to help Norman were skilled workers—people who understood what needed to be done to bring in the harvest.

Jesus doesn't necessarily need all skilled workers to bring in his harvest. He is looking for workers with two key qualities.

Workers Who Will Pray

Jesus needs workers who will pray for the harvest and, in particular, workers who will "ask the Lord of the harvest . . . to send out workers into his harvest field" (Luke 10:2).

I find this directive interesting. Why does Jesus want to be asked to send out more workers into his harvest field? Why do we need to ask him to do what we already know he wants to do?

Well, I'm not really sure, but I have three guesses.

Maybe he wants to know that we want lost people to be saved as much as he does.

Maybe he wants to know we know that without him, the Lord of the harvest, there would be no harvest.

Maybe he wants us to ask him to send workers because it confirms we understand that we can't do this by ourselves.

You can't reach this world for Jesus. I can't reach this world for Jesus.

But we can reach this world for Jesus with the Lord's help.

As we urgently work together to bring in the harvest, we must pray—trusting that the Lord will send out others to join us.

Workers Who Will Go

After asking his workers to pray, Jesus then emphatically commands them—and us—to go (Luke 10:3). Serving Jesus is not a stationary experience. The world revolves around Jesus, but it doesn't revolve around us. We can't just stand where we are, all self-important, and wait for the lost to find us to get the help they need. Though sometimes Jesus sends the lost to us individually or sends the lost to the church building, he expects the church (us) to go and find lost people. Obedience to Jesus, the Lord of the harvest, requires a willingness to go—which makes sense, because fish don't just jump into the boat and fields don't just harvest themselves.

The best way to reach people for Christ—in my opinion— is to go to where they are and share Jesus with them. Inviting people to come to church is good, but inviting ourselves into the world is better!

Jesus, knowing that time was of the essence, didn't command the world to come to his disciples; he commanded his disciples to go to the world. When he sent out the twelve, he said, "Go . . . to the lost sheep of Israel" (Matthew 10:6).

To explain the banquet he's going to host in heaven, Jesus told a parable in which a servant is ordered to "go out quickly into the streets and alleys of the town and bring in the poor, the crippled, the blind and the lame" and then to "go out to the roads and country lanes and compel them to come in, so that my house will be full" (Luke 14:21, 23). Jesus clearly wants people to come into his house. We want that too, which is why we invite people to come to church (it's what we're used to and what we've done for many years). But I think there's a better way to reach lost people. I think it's better for you and me to go where people are and show them the love of Jesus through intentional relationships in which we introduce them to him.

When he was preparing to ascend to heaven, Jesus left his disciples with this commission: "Go and make disciples of all nations" (Matthew 28:19-20). So we must keep inviting, but we must also keep going—quickly, into the streets and alleys of our towns—to fill Jesus' house properly.

We must go to them, we must reach them, and we must do it now. The harvest is not over. We must not have Thanksgiving too soon. As Robert Moffat said, "We have all eternity to celebrate our victories, but only one short hour before sunset in which to win them."[9]

We must have a sense of urgency to go and reach lost people while we can.

That's what Captain Sully understood.

When his plane came to a stop in the middle of the Hudson River, another alarm went off in Sully's head. He knew he had to get everyone off the plane as quickly as possible. Immediately, the crew began evacuating passengers onto the wings and into inflated slides while the plane began to sink, floating down the river with the current. When it seemed that every passenger was safely out of the plane, Sully did an amazing thing.

With a sense of urgency, because the plane was taking on water, he walked the length of the cabin of the plane to make sure that every passenger was out of the plane—not once, but twice![10] After making sure that everyone else was safely out, Sully exited too.

That's what Jesus would have done. That's what Jesus has done.

Jesus, with a sense of urgency, has sent us out into the harvest fields to make sure that everyone has the chance to be brought safely home. We must walk through our neighborhoods, our workplaces, our communities, and our homes as many times as it takes to make sure that everyone has the opportunity to get safely off this planet.

The world is sinking. The alarm is sounding. The harvest is plentiful. Let's get to work now, because it's later than it ever was.

FINDING A SENSE OF URGENCY

- Write the name of one lost person you want to reach for Jesus.

- List one thing you can do this week to start reaching that person for Jesus.

- Stop right now and pray that the Lord will send more workers into the harvest field. After entreating the Lord, ask him what role he would have you play in this.

9
MERCY

Which of these three do you think was a neighbor to
the man who fell into the hands of robbers?

LUKE 10:36

I once heard *grace* defined as "giving someone something
that person doesn't deserve." (We talked about grace in chapter 3.) The same person defined *mercy* as "not giving someone
something that person does deserve."

We tend to like it when people get what they deserve.

Take this morning, for example. I'm sitting here with a
hot cup of coffee with lots of cream and sugar, in my comfortable pajamas, with my beautiful wife and children resting
peacefully down the hall and downstairs. Through the window next to me, I can see the dawn of a fantastic day. The sky
is an uninterrupted proclamation of beauty and brilliance in
a captivating shade of blue. The sun is rising behind me, and

I can't see it yet, but its rays are touching the trees across the street—announcing its pending arrival by lighting them up with golden radiance. A small, brown bird just landed on the porch rail outside my window. I smile as I watch him jitter nervously on his perch—looking around as if he's being pursued or maybe had too much caffeine. A jogger just ran by with her faithful yellow Labrador leading the way. The world is waking up and the day promises to be glorious—so why do I so desperately want the preacher I just watched on YouTube to get throat-punched? This legalist recorded himself telling kids waiting in line to see Santa that there is no Santa Claus and that their parents are liars.[1]

What is wrong with me? As a Christian, shouldn't I be a little concerned about his ministry and relationship with Jesus? Shouldn't I want someone, somewhere, somehow to share the love of Jesus with him? Aren't I the worst person in the world because I passionately despise everything about that guy—in Christian love?

Why do I want someone in his general vicinity to shut him up, ram some mistletoe down his throat, or summon a security guard to tase him?

Why do I want someone to take revenge on him for what he is doing to those little kids' dreams and hopes of Santa?

REVENGE!

We love revenge. It brings us pleasure. We taste it; we like it; we want more.

Revenge sells books. It's the major plot point of most

blockbuster movies. We love when the witch melts, when the Death Star explodes, when Rocky knocks out Ivan Drago, when Scar is killed by the hyenas. And we're right with Inigo Montoya in *The Princess Bride* when he finally confronts the six-fingered man and says, "You killed my father. Prepare to die." Aah, sweet revenge!

I know these stories are just make-believe, but the pleasure vengeance brings me is nothing but real and completely satisfying. What is wrong with me? What is wrong with us? Jesus clearly taught that we are not supposed to seek revenge but must trust God for justice: "Do not resist an evil person. If anyone slaps you on the right cheek, turn to them the other cheek also. And if anyone wants to sue you and take your shirt, hand over your coat as well. If anyone forces you to go one mile, go with them two miles. . . . Love your enemies and pray for those who persecute you" (Matthew 5:39-41, 44).

Revenge, at first though sweet, bitter ere long back on itself recoils.

—JOHN MILTON

When was the last time you prayed for the president for whom you did not vote? For the friend you don't speak to anymore because she hurt your feelings? For your ex-wife? When was the last time you prayed for the boss who fired you six months before you would have been eligible for full retirement benefits? When was the last time you prayed for your neighbors?

Jesus would be praying, and did pray, for his abusers, because Jesus is merciful.

Mercy doesn't sell a lot of books or movie tickets, and it may not make you popular at the Pentagon or as a UFC competitor, but it reflects the heart of God and it's an essential ingredient to any meaningful effort to reach lost people for Jesus.

Jesus told an important parable about mercy.

Now, a parable can be a trap. Jesus told parables because they are powerful teaching tools. You think you're hearing a sweet little story about a pearl, and then—snap!—you realize that Jesus was really talking about the Kingdom of Heaven. That simple story of a farmer scattering seed? Out of nowhere—snap!—you realize that Jesus was not talking about seeds at all, but about his teachings and you. You think you're hearing a sad tale about a lost sheep when—snap!—you realize that Jesus is explaining how much he loves lost people.

You think Luke 10:25-37 tells a tale about a Good Samaritan, but—snap!—it's really a story about mercy.

THE QUESTION

An expert on the law came to Jesus with an important question: "Teacher . . . what must I do to inherit eternal life?" (Luke 10:25).

Jesus replied with a question about what was written in God's law.

The legal expert answered, "'Love the Lord your God with all your heart and with all your soul and with all your strength and with all your mind'; and, 'Love your neighbor as yourself'" (Luke 10:27).

Jesus stated that this answer was correct. "Do this and you will live," he advised (Luke 10:28).

Which prompted this legalist to ask an all-important question: "And who is my neighbor?" (Luke 10:29).

Our salvation is not about what we do or have done, but about what God has done for us.

"Love the LORD your God," from Deuteronomy 6:5, was one of the best-known commands in the Jewish Scriptures. The Jews recited this every morning and evening. They carried it around in their phylacteries. But "Love your neighbor as yourself," from Leviticus 19:18, not so much.

When Jesus used the word *neighbor*, he wasn't talking about the people who live next door to us. That would be too easy. Wouldn't it be wonderful if we could please Jesus and prove our loyalty to God simply by loving the people who live on either side of our houses? Instead, we're going to see that when Jesus talked about loving our neighbor, he was making a broader and completely different point from what we usually think. More on that a little later.

The legal expert who went to Jesus was concerned about what he needed to do to inherit eternal life, which I have to stop and commend, because it seems to me that way too many people could not care less about what is going to happen to them when they die. But I also would caution him about thinking that there is anything we can actually do to inherit eternal life. The cool thing about an inheritance is that you don't have to do anything to receive it—it's a gift from a parent to a child. Like many of us, this guy has it all wrong. Our salvation is not about what we do or have done, but about what God has done for us.

Jesus' answer to this man's question was revolutionary.

THE ANSWER

Jesus answered this legal expert's question with a parable that has a cast of characters like the start of a joke you would have heard at a synagogue two millennia ago: "Okay, a priest, a Levite, and a Samaritan were walking down the road . . ."

In Jesus' parable (Luke 10:30-37), a man was robbed, stripped, beaten, and left for dead as he went down from Jerusalem to Jericho. As he lay there dying, a priest and a Levite passed by the man on the other side of the road, but then a Samaritan came to where the man was: "And when he saw him, he took pity on him. He went to him and bandaged his wounds, pouring on oil and wine. Then he put the man on his own donkey, brought him to an inn, and took care of him. The next day he took out two denarii and gave them to the innkeeper. 'Look after him,' he said, 'and when I return, I will reimburse you for any extra expense you may have'" (verses 33-35).

By stating that this man was going down from Jerusalem to Jericho, Jesus seemed to imply that the man was Jewish. That's significant because the only person to stop and help the man was the only person in the story who wasn't Jewish.

The priest should have stopped. Priests were the descendants of Aaron and had specific charge of the temple worship. This priest was something like a preacher. The Levite should have stopped. Levites were the descendants of Levi and performed the tasks necessary for maintaining the temple, preparing offerings, and assisting with worship. When you think of this Levite, think of an important deacon or a key ministry leader in your church.

The men in this story, based on the knowledge they had and based on the fact that they were supposed to be serving God, should have been the most likely prospects to provide for the needs of this injured man. True knowledge of God should result in true love for God and for his people.

Now, they may have had some good excuses for not stopping.

They may have been too busy. *You know, it can get really complicated trying to help someone, so it's probably best to just keep moving along. I need to get home and spend quality time watching TV with my family.*

They may have had no training to help an injured man. *I've never had CPR training, and he might have some kind of virus. I can't risk catching a disease from a stranger, because I have to sing a special at church on Sunday!*

They may have thought that this man was too far gone and nothing could be done to help him. *Sometimes you just have to let nature run its course—you know, survival of the fittest and all that. Who am I to suggest it's not his time to go? Better to leave it in God's hands, I say.*

Maybe it was just too dangerous for them to risk stopping to help. *I've never been in this part of town after dark. I can't risk my safety. What would my wife and kids do if something happened to me? I'm sure someone else will come by who is better equipped, like one of those guys in the red berets, you know, the Guardian Angels. They're trained for stuff like this.*

Whatever their excuses, these two Jewish religious leaders in Jesus' story did not stop to help another Jew but left him to die. Only a Samaritan stopped to help.

The Jews hated Samaritans. In 721 BC, Sargon of Assyria had invaded and destroyed Samaria. He carried all but a remnant of the Jewish population away to captivity. Those who remained intermarried with the Assyrians, creating a mixed race hated by the Jews, who considered them unclean. So when you think of the Good Samaritan, think of someone viewed as less than human by pretty much everyone—someone like a Taliban leader, an IRS agent, or the inventor of e-mail spam.

This Samaritan is the hero of Jesus' story. He didn't stop to question whether the man on the road was his neighbor. No, he simply acted because he felt sorry for the injured man. He bandaged the man's wounds, put him on his donkey, took him to an inn, and cared for him there. He didn't desert him but went the extra mile and even paid for the man's housing expenses. He then promised to come back and pay the innkeeper for any other expenses the man might have.

How many injured people did we pass by on the roads we traveled this week? Did you go to the other side of the road when you saw someone struggling through divorce, abuse, an unexpected pregnancy, alcohol or drug addiction, pornography, homosexuality, or a terminal illness?

Jesus ended his story with another question: "Which of these three do you think was a neighbor to the man who fell into the hands of robbers?" (Luke 10:36).

Whoa! What happened there? That's not the answer the expert in the law was expecting. Hadn't he asked Jesus, "And who is my neighbor?" Now Jesus had turned it all around into a question for the questioner—because the expert in the law had asked the wrong question. His circle was very small, and he hoped to keep it that way. We can almost hear him thinking, *Okay. I get it. My neighbor is someone like that hurt man. I just need to make sure I help people like that whenever I come across them, which isn't very often, so this isn't going to be that bad.*

Jesus blew up his circle—and his delusions—by telling him that the answer to his question was not the man in need, but the Samaritan.

A neighbor is not determined by geography, culture, race, or any other bond. A true neighbor is anyone who rises above all barriers and selfishness to help anyone in need. Jesus told the expert in the law to be like the Samaritan.

Snap!

My friend Travis will associate with anybody, especially his neighbors. I've never met anyone more skilled at reaching his neighbors for Christ. Travis doesn't care who they are or how loud their dog barks after ten o'clock at night. He moved into a neighborhood south of Orlando, and within a year he'd led several of his neighbors to Christ simply by associating with them and showing them mercy. There were—as there are with all neighbors—situations that he could have let escalate into barriers between his neighbors and himself, but that's not how Travis lives. Shortly after Travis moved in, his neighbors discovered that a Christian had moved in, not a judge.

The religious leaders in Jesus' day were not willing to associate with the kind of people whom Jesus spent time with. Jesus accepted extreme poverty and hardship so that he might

A Good Samaritan Dad

My dad was a preacher with a huge, generous heart that didn't know many boundaries, so his love for God and passion for the lost often played out in unorthodox ways—at least by most standards.

Dad took seriously the mandate to meet the needs of "the least of these" (Matthew 25:45) and to show hospitality—and yes, Mom was in on this too—because in doing so we might be entertaining angels without knowing it (Hebrews 13:2). So neighbors, family, friends, missionaries, and strangers often sat at our table (or in our yard, eating watermelon and cantaloupe).

One Saturday morning, my brothers and I awoke to find that Dad had brought home a stranger. Late Friday night, after preaching at a church a couple of hours away, as he drove home on Highway 50 in a pouring rain, he had picked up a hitchhiker.

My brothers and I were intrigued by Rich, a tall, skinny guy who was traveling home from someplace in Missouri to northern Indiana after having been in prison for five years. He carried only a small bag. I don't remember his face, but I do recall that he had part of a finger missing on his left hand and wore a ring on the little finger of his right—a particularly engaging feature, as you don't see many men in southern Illinois with pinky rings.

Dad planned to buy a bus ticket to help Rich complete his

journey more securely. However, as Saturday wore on, Rich seemed content to stay for the day, and we were pleased for him to be there. He sat with us at our table. He stayed Saturday night, went to church with us on Sunday, met all the good folk at our small country church, spent a third night on a couch in the basement, and then went with Dad to the bus station on Monday morning.

Throughout that weekend, we did our usual stuff—playing in the front yard, riding bicycles, eating, singing around the table, and just visiting. Yes, there was talk about faith. Rich fought against a really cynical view of the world—and of Christians as well.

I'd like to share some incredible ending to the story of Rich, the stranger—but God knows his life's journey. We never saw him again. When Dad returned from the bus station, I asked him if he was ever scared about picking up a stranger. I was twelve years old, and even back then, people were generally starting to have boundaries about things like that. But Dad wasn't plagued with a lot of the what-ifs of life. For him, it was really simple—and clear. He said, "Well, sweetie, I just know that's what Jesus would have done."

—TWILA—

spend his life's energy in the homes of the poor, the unfortunate, the sick, and the sinful.

Like the Samaritan, Jesus was merciful to people regardless of who they were, what they'd done, or whether they liked him.

As we eat with sinners, we must flavor each meal with mercy.

Leave the judgment at home.

Give wrath the night off.

Tell hypocrisy that you've made other plans. Mercy is on the menu tonight.

It's what everyone deserves. And you want people to get what they deserve . . . right?

TAKING STEPS TO BE MORE MERCIFUL

- List three people you don't like very much.

- Beside each person's name, list one positive quality you've noticed in that person's life.

- Pray for each person by name, asking God to bless him or her abundantly.

10

HUMILITY

All those who exalt themselves will be humbled, and
those who humble themselves will be exalted.

LUKE 14:11

I love country music. And since Jesus was born in a barn, I'm pretty sure that he does too. Country songs have some of the best titles. Here are a few of my favorites:

- "How Can I Miss You If You Won't Go Away?"
- "I Bought the Shoes That Just Walked Out on Me"
- "I Changed Her Oil, She Changed My Life"
- "I'd Rather Pass a Kidney Stone Than Another Night with You"
- "If the Phone Doesn't Ring, It's Me"

The thing I love about country music is that so many of its themes speak to real troubles that trouble real people:

trouble with love, trouble at work, trouble with your mother-in-law, trouble with your bar stool, trouble with your tractor, trouble with the tattoo that you found on your face when you woke up after that night at the county fair, trouble with your three girlfriends, trouble with the one tooth you've got left, trouble with your truck, trouble with your dog, and trouble with discovering that you're your own grandpa.

One song title in particular resonates with me because it addresses something that troubles me daily: "Oh Lord, It's Hard to Be Humble," written and performed by Mac Davis.

Sometimes it is hard to be humble.

Humility is the quality of having a modest view of one's person, rank, and importance.

William Beebe, the naturalist, occasionally visited the home of former president Teddy Roosevelt. President Roosevelt and Beebe would go out at night to find in the starry sky a bright spot near the Great Square of Pegasus constellation. One of them would say, "That is the Spiral Galaxy in Andromeda. It is as large as our Milky Way. It is one of a hundred million galaxies. It consists of one hundred billion suns, each larger than our sun." Then President Roosevelt would smile and tell Beebe, "Now I think we are small enough! Let's go to bed."[1]

My friend Brent gave me great advice about humility that I think about almost every day. He told me that I should take humility wherever I can find it. Teddy Roosevelt found humility by looking at the stars. Jesus found humility by looking "to the interests of the others" (see Philippians 2:4)—ours. I find humility by looking at the cross.

The cross is the essence of humility.

The purpose of the cross was to humiliate and then kill its victim. Stripped of everything, hanging for all to see and mock, the person who hung high on a cross was as low as a human being could be. A man on a cross was nothing— nothing but a criminal, nothing but a visual reminder of the consequences of upsetting the Romans, nothing but a warning sign, nothing but an example, nothing but nothing.

The apostle Paul reflected, "Have the same mindset as Christ Jesus: Who, being in very nature God, did not consider equality with God something to be used to his own advantage; rather, he made himself *nothing* by taking the very nature of a servant, being made in human likeness. And being found in appearance as a man, he *humbled himself* by becoming obedient to death—even death on a cross!" (Philippians 2:5-8, emphasis added).

Why did Jesus make himself nothing?

So we all could be something. The cross was not the end but the beginning of something amazing. It was the beginning of hope. It was the beginning of forgiveness. It was the beginning of grace.

The most important part of the gospel, which Paul passed on "as of first importance," begins with the fact that "Christ died for our sins" (1 Corinthians 15:3). So if Christ had not died for our sins, he could not have been buried, could not have been raised on the third day, could not have appeared to people (verses 4-6), and could not raise us from the dead too. With Paul I affirm, "If Christ has not been raised, our preaching is useless and so is your faith" (verse 14). So praise

God that Christ did indeed die for our sins, was buried in a borrowed tomb, did rise from the dead on the third day, did appear to people, and has conquered death so that you and I can—in Jesus—be raised from our first death never to die again! Jesus went to the cross in humility so that all sinners could leave the cross with confidence.

The cross was not the end but the beginning of something amazing.

As we eat with sinners, it would be wise to start each meal with a slice of humble pie, because it seems to me that it's too easy to position ourselves safely on a comfortable perch and look down with pity on those so far below us. This is absurd and un-Christlike. If we really want to reach lost people, we must be humble—and true humility comes from standing next to the cross.

That being said, since it's so hard to be humble, let's use an acronym that might help: HARD.

H—HEALING IS PERPETUALLY POSSIBLE WITH JESUS

One Sabbath, Jesus went to eat with a prominent Pharisee (Luke 14:1-24). The Pharisees and experts in the law at the meal watched Jesus carefully. They were fascinated with what Jesus said and what he did. He didn't respect the boundaries they set—and counted on—to protect their most sacred beliefs. Jesus seemed to have no boundaries. He had intimate relationships with people the Pharisees and experts in the law viewed as inappropriate. None of this made sense to these legalists.

In my first book, *Running on Empty*, I point out that the problem with legalists is not that they love the law too much but that they love people too little.[2] The Pharisees, watching Jesus from their prideful perch, were legalists who didn't love people enough. This is evident in their reaction to Jesus' healing of the man who suffered from dropsy.[3] When they saw Jesus heal this man, they should have been praising God. They should have been shouting, "Hosanna! Blessed is he who comes in the name of the Lord!" They should have been slapping Jesus high fives and saying things like "That's what ol' dropsy gets for bringin' its sorry self into the presence of our Messiah!" Instead, they were silent. Not a single word. Not a peep.

From the context in Luke 14, it appears that this man had been planted in front of Jesus as a pass-or-fail test. According to the law, the Sabbath was a day of rest, not work. It seems the Pharisees wanted to see whether Jesus would help this man and violate their understanding of the Sabbath law.

This is all so sad to me.

The man was suffering, and these legalists couldn't answer a simple question: "Is it lawful to heal on the Sabbath or not?" (Luke 14:3). New Testament historian R. C. Foster pointed out some of the irony in this situation: "The Pharisees claimed to be the specialists of the day at answering just such questions, but they were afraid to answer this one. They did not want to give an affirmative answer, and they were afraid to give a negative one."[4] I think the answer for their no answer is obvious: They didn't say a word because they didn't care about this poor guy. He needed healing, but these legalists could only think about themselves and tripping up Jesus.

God save us from prideful legalists!

Well, God did save this guy from these prideful legalists. Jesus, the designer of the human body and author of the Sabbath law, humbly healed this nameless man and then asked the Pharisees and experts in the law another question: "If one of you has a child or an ox that falls into a well on the Sabbath day, will you not immediately pull it out?" (Luke 14:5).

Silence.

What is your answer to that question?

A—ALWAYS REMEMBER THE WELL

I don't have an ox, but I do have children whom I love passionately. If any of them fell into a well, you'd have to forcibly restrain me to keep me from doing everything I could to get them out. I know you would do the same thing. When "Baby Jessica" McClure was trapped in a well in Midland, Texas, for almost fifty-nine hours back in 1987, people all over the world sat captivated by TV screens, hoping and praying for her rescue, and we celebrated as one when we saw that little bandaged girl being carried to safety.[5]

We must listen as they cry out from the depths, desperate for us to hear them and come to their rescue.

What loving first-century Jewish father wouldn't rescue his child from a well on the Sabbath? We all know the answer, but that's not the point, because these legalists weren't interested in rescuing anyone; they were only interested in trapping Jesus.

People are pawns to legalists, and the guy with dropsy meant less to them than an ox.

He meant more to Jesus than anything. You mean more to Jesus than anything.

Sinners mean more to Jesus than anything.

How would you answer this question? "If one of you has a friend, a neighbor, or a coworker who falls into sin on any day of the week, will you not immediately pull that person out?"

No silence, please.

We all know the answer, and that's my point.

There are people trapped all around us—people who need help, people who need hope, people who need healing. We must listen as they cry out from the depths, desperate for us to hear them and come to their rescue.

Perhaps too many of us have forgotten what it feels like to be trapped in that well. Our rescue may have come twenty, thirty, or forty years ago, and even though we may still carry the scars of the ordeal, we've forgotten what it is like to feel hopeless, helpless, and doomed.

We were broken back then. We were reachable back then, teachable. We were humble back when we were rescued from that well, but now the well is only a faint memory of the pitiful person each of us was so long ago—a memory kept in a dark, unvisited corner of our minds.

With sincerity and a strong desire to maintain purity in our spiritual walk, we resolve in our testimonies at church never to go back to the well, which is good because we need to stay away from sin—but it is also bad because there are people at our old wells who still need salvation. We must not allow the pride we feel in our new lives—as weak sinners who have now become overcomers through Christ—to lead us to forget the sinners we left behind at the well.

With true humility, Jesus resolves never to leave the well until every last person who is willing to follow him is rescued.

Christlike humility requires that we never forget the well and those trapped inside it. None of us is too good, too holy, too important, too successful, too prominent in our denomination, too valuable to our church board, too recognizable from our television ministry, too anything to help hurting people out of the well. We're all just former wellions (my word for people who used to be trapped in a physical or spiritual well), so let's get over ourselves, get down from our ivory towers, and humbly get back to the well—there are plenty of people who need to be pulled out!

R—RESEAT YOURSELF IF NECESSARY

Every table has chief seats—seats where the most important, prominent, and valued guests sit. It was customary in the first century for the host to assign guests to seats of honor, but in Luke 14:7 Jesus found the guests scrambling to secure the most prominent seats for themselves.

One Sunday a few years ago, my sister visited a church for the first time. She'd been having a rough morning. She's a strong Christian, and she knew that she really needed to be in church around other Christians—especially on a morning like this.

Well, she walked in a few minutes before the service and couldn't find a seat. Then she spotted a seat close to the front on the right side. She made the long walk down the side aisle and started to sit down, but the woman in the pew said, "This seat's saved."

Feeling slightly embarrassed now that she was all the way up front with no place to go, my sister sweetly said, "No problem," and proceeded toward the back of the section, looking for another seat.

She found one a few rows back, but the nicely dressed older man sitting closest to the spot looked her way and whispered, "We're saving this seat."

Undeterred, my sister continued farther to the back, with a little more urgency because she could hear the worship service beginning. Finally, she saw an open spot on the back row and made her way there as quickly as she could. Surprise . . . that seat was indeed saved too.

My sister was so upset that she walked out the back door with tears streaming down her face. She sat in her car and sobbed, brokenhearted.

This is about more than just the chief seats in our churches; I'm also talking about the chief seats in life. It's sad when we take the chief seats in our church buildings and expect other Christians to accommodate us, but it's even sadder when we do the same thing to lost people outside our church buildings by expecting them to come to Christ on our terms. Are we more concerned about saving the chief seats for ourselves, or saving souls?

Terry Reyes doesn't expect people to come to Christ on his terms. If he had terms, they might have been that lost people would come to Christ by way of the Sunday morning church service and be properly dressed, clean, and free of foul language. But praise God, he was willing to give up his preferences, his comfort, and his seat so that he could save more souls.

We are not playing musical chairs, where survival depends on grabbing the best seat possible before the music stops.

Terry Reyes's heart broke for the plight of homeless people on the streets of Manhattan. He'd felt God's call to come to the United States from the Philippines as a missionary to reach American Filipinos for Christ, but he realized God had different plans when his first convert was a Jewish woman. Terry was serving faithfully in Hell's Kitchen, but he felt that he was serving at a "safe distance" from those he was called to help. He fed them, clothed them, and ministered to them, but at the end of each day he went home to sleep in a comfortable bed in his own home.

One day, sensing God's leading, Terry decided to leave "his seat" at night to be with those homeless people who were unable to find a place in a local shelter. For almost a year Terry spent every Tuesday night sleeping on the streets with the homeless people on United Nations Avenue in front of the United Nations Building. On the street he experienced what his people experienced—being cold, feeling uncomfortable, being driven away by the police, and even being robbed of his new tennis shoes and forced to walk the streets of New York in his socks. Being on the street wasn't winning people to Christ on Terry's terms but on God's terms.

Terry didn't have to sleep on the street with homeless people to help them. He was already helping—and doing it well. Terry started sleeping on the street because he felt God's call to do so. Terry faithfully obeyed and ended up being used by God to bring many street people to Jesus.

Terry knows that we are not playing musical chairs, where survival depends on grabbing the best seat possible before the music stops. But sometimes it appears that's what we're playing in the church. Relationship evangelism is not a game we win by pushing others out of the way. No, this is not a game at all. This is a matter of spiritual life and death, and we must humble ourselves, give up the chief seats at the table of life, take the worst seats for ourselves, and make room for those who are yet to enjoy the blessings of the feast. After all, "all those who exalt themselves will be humbled, and those who humble themselves will be exalted" (Luke 14:11).

D—DINNER SHOULD BE A PARTY TO WHICH EVERYONE IS INVITED!

When we find it hard to be humble, we must remember that life in Jesus is supposed to be an amazing party to which everyone is invited.

The best parties I've ever been to are pictures of sacrifice. At the best parties, it's obvious the host sacrificed time, energy, and money purely for the benefit of one person or a group of people.

Jesus had the same take on parties. He said that the best parties are not self-serving but others-serving and that, if we are willing to sacrifice for others, we "will be blessed" beyond our wildest imaginations (Luke 14:14).

Let me introduce you to someone who understands exactly what Jesus was trying to teach this Pharisee and us. Meet Katie Hosking.

Katie had an amazing party planned—and she was the guest of honor because it was her wedding reception. Katie and her parents were expecting 150 guests at The Golf Club at Echo Falls in Snohomish, Washington. Her parents had made the reservations, paid the deposits—everything was all set, when the unexpected happened: Katie decided to call off her wedding only twelve days before she was supposed to be married. Club policy required full payment for any event canceled less than sixty days before the scheduled date, so Katie and her parents were going to lose a lot of money. This is when an ordinary party became an extraordinary party.

Katie's mother reported that once she and her husband "got past the panic," they took a suggestion from her brother-in-law and decided to invite the staff and residents of a local homeless shelter to share in the evening. Katie's family was joined by about forty homeless people and staff from the shelter. Besides the festive atmosphere of a full-fledged party—DJ and dancing included—the homeless guests at Katie's party were treated to a feast that included baron of

A Pilot's Mission

I'm a pilot, and I've made it my mission to help people as often as I can in the cities I visit. Once as I was walking back to my hotel in downtown Seattle, a guy in his early twenties asked for a handout. I don't normally give change, but if asked I will almost always buy a meal. Sometimes I have time to sit and chat, and in this case I did. I asked the young man what he was doing there.

He was trying to make it on his own from Portland, had spent a few months trying to keep small jobs but just wasn't able to do it, and was working his way back to a different part of Washington to get to his brother. He thanked me for the food and commented on how many people would have turned him down.

I felt that if he'd had money, he would have bought someone else a meal too. I've long understood that I can't help everybody, but it's nice to have opportunities like this when I can help somebody.

—JOHN—

beef, salmon, shrimp cocktail, fettuccine, fruit, and straw-berry shortcake for dessert.

Katie's mother described one of the highlights of the eve-ning: "One homeless woman got her son out of a wheelchair, took that child out on the dance floor and picked him up and danced with him. It was a beautiful sight. Our kids realized that even when something bad happens, somebody else has something worse. It was an eye-opener."[6]

Katie had every right to think about herself on what was to have been her wedding day. She was hurt, she was sad, and no one would have blamed her if she spent June 18, 2005, curled up on her couch with a box of tissues, hosting a well-deserved pity party, but that's not what she did. She did what Jesus would have done. She humbled herself, thought of other people, invited them to the party, and gave them an experience they will never forget.

We can do what Katie did if we will only think HARD and humble ourselves:

- H—Healing is perpetually possible with Jesus.
- A—Always remember the well.
- R—Reseat yourself if necessary.
- D—Dinner should be a party to which everyone is invited!

Augustine said, "Should you ask me: What is the first thing in religion? I should reply: The first, second, and third thing therein is humility."

Think HARD about that.

I think we are small enough now, so I'm going to bed.

MAKING GUESTS FEEL MORE WELCOME IN CHURCH

- Reserve seating in the back of each section for guests.

- Have the worship leader regularly instruct members to make room for guests—giving up their seats if need be.

- Place greeters in the sanctuary whose only job is to seek out and welcome guests.

11
INVESTMENT

Whoever does not carry their cross and
follow me cannot be my disciple.

LUKE 14:27

In preparation for writing this chapter, I've read the four-teenth chapter of Luke a half dozen times, and every time I read it I get more and more frustrated with the Pharisees, religious hypocrites, and the church.

Read the Parable of the Great Banquet in Luke 14 and the verses that come before it, and you'll understand my angst. I'm serious. Put this book down, read Luke 14:1-24, and then come back.

See what I'm talking about?

I have no idea what he looked like—and this may be really unfair—but based on the context, when I picture the guy who said, "Blessed is the one who will eat at the feast in the kingdom of God" (Luke 14:15), I picture some large, clueless Pharisee. He's nicely dressed in a flowing robe, reclining on one arm, and in the hand of his other arm is a sizable leg of lamb from which he's just taken a bite that's too big. So he's forced to speak out of the corner of his full mouth, sending bits of lamb flying through the air as he spouts his "blessing."

Then Jesus, wiping some of that lamb off his face (I know it doesn't say this, but go with me here), tells a story that should be hard for any self-righteous, self-indulgent hypocrite to swallow.

A man was having a great banquet, and he sent a servant out to let his invited guests know that everything was ready, but all of them started making excuses.

One said he had just bought a field and needed to go see it. He bought a field without seeing it? What a lame excuse. Another said he had purchased five yoke of oxen and was on his way to try them out. He bought oxen without trying them out first? Give me a break. Still another said he couldn't come because he'd just been married. Okay, this is a pretty good excuse, but the other two? Pitiful.

An old military man once told me that excuses are like armpits: Everyone has a couple, and they all stink. These excuses stunk, so when the servant went back to his master with the news, the master was ticked off and ordered his servant to go back out into the streets and alleys of the town and bring in the poor, the crippled, the blind, and the lame.

When the servant reported that he had already done that but there was still room, the master replied, "Go out to the roads and country lanes and compel them to come in, so that my house will be full" (Luke 14:23).

We've already pointed out in this book that Jesus wants a full house. He doesn't want anyone left out. How full is your church? Any room for a few more? Of course. There's plenty of room for lost people in our church buildings; that's not the problem. The problem is that there aren't enough of us resolved to bring in the harvest.

Now back to the story.

Then (I know it doesn't say this either, but humor me . . . it could have happened) I picture Jesus looking at the guy who made the blessing and saying—as the room gets completely silent, "I tell you, not one of those who were invited will get a taste of my banquet" (Luke 14:24).

Gulp. Cue the dramatic music and tight shot on the Pharisees' mouths as they stop chewing.

Interestingly, Jesus told parables to make clear points. His point in telling this parable was to issue a warning to every listener that it's a mistake to talk about how great the blessings of the Kingdom will be if, in fact, you yourself are rejecting God's invitation through Jesus and making it difficult for others to join the party as well.

Earlier Jesus witnessed these religious leaders fighting for the best seats at the dinner table (Luke 14:7). He knew that these same men—so concerned about securing the best seats for themselves—had no concern that the poor, the crippled, the lame, and the blind had yet to be invited to the banquet.

The Pharisees didn't get it. They ignored their responsibility. The Pharisees were supposed to protect the poor, the crippled, the lame, and

Excuses are like armpits: Everyone has a couple, and they all stink.

the blind. The Lord had made it clear how he wanted those kinds of people to be treated:

- Do not curse the deaf or put a stumbling block in front of the blind, but fear your God. I am the LORD (Leviticus 19:14).

- If any of your fellow Israelites become poor and are unable to support themselves among you, help them as you would a foreigner and stranger, so they can continue to live among you (Leviticus 25:35).

- There will always be poor people in the land. Therefore I command you to be openhanded toward your fellow Israelites who are poor and needy in your land (Deuteronomy 15:11).

- "Because the poor are plundered and the needy groan, I will now arise," says the LORD. "I will protect them from those who malign them" (Psalm 12:5).

The Pharisees were supposed to make sure that the poor and needy made it into God's banquet safely. Instead, they were fighting over the chief seats. If only they would follow Jesus' example!

JESUS WAS FULLY INVESTED IN REACHING LOST PEOPLE

Hosting a party for a full house is a big investment.

When my wife and I hosted a simple birthday party for our daughter Payton and ten of her friends, we were fully invested in making sure that her thirteenth birthday party was a success. Our simple party still required a huge investment of time and a significant investment of money.

The great banquet in the parable is like the great banquet in heaven that Jesus will host for all who have responded to his invitation. To host that party in heaven, Jesus first will have to make some investments.

An Investment of His Energy

A great banquet in Jesus' day required a huge investment of energy on the part of the host. The home had to be prepared. The guests had to be invited—twice, because people didn't have watches and needed a second invitation to know when the feast was ready. The food had to be prepared—from scratch. The wine needed at least forty days to be properly fermented.

Jesus was obviously talking about the Kingdom of Heaven here, and we know, from what he told the disciples, that he was investing all his energy in preparing the Kingdom for his followers. Jesus told his disciples that when he left he was going to "prepare a place" for them (John 14:2)—which means that heaven is going to be amazing, because Jesus never does anything halfway.

We know that Jesus is sparing no expense in preparing our heavenly banquet.

An Investment of His Resources

This kind of banquet in Jesus' day would also have required a huge investment of the host's resources. A host in this situation would have spared no expense to make sure that every need of every guest was fully met, and we know that Jesus is sparing no expense in preparing our heavenly banquet. He promised that every faithful attendee is going to receive treasure in heaven (see Matthew 6:20). Do you know how incredible something has to be to be considered a treasure in a place with streets of gold, mansions, and a crystal sea? Wow!

An Investment of His Life

Because we know that this parable is about the banquet that will occur in the Kingdom of Heaven, we understand that the party we'll experience in heaven required an investment of the very life of Jesus. All gain access to the heavenly banquet only through the death of the host. Yes, entrance to this banquet is free to all except the host and the host's servants.

What?

Yes, I did say that this banquet is going to cost us something too.

WE MUST BE FULLY INVESTED IN REACHING LOST PEOPLE

Jesus attracted large crowds of people, which didn't mean too much to Jesus from a popularity standpoint. Jesus wasn't interested in being popular; he was interested only in making sure lost people had a seat at the banquet. Some people were following Jesus for the show. They wanted to see signs and wonders. Jesus called them "wicked" (Luke 11:29). He wants his followers to understand that being his disciple is not about entertainment but about investment.

An Investment of Our Energy

Jesus told the crowds of people following him that being his disciple is like building a tower. A ton of energy and commitment is required to finish building a tower, and it's best to count the cost before you start: "For if you lay the foundation and are not able to finish it, everyone who sees it will ridicule you" (Luke 14:29).

We have a big job to do, and we need to be committed to doing the hard work required for finishing the job in a way that brings honor and glory to God.

There's a building next to I-4 in Orlando that the press and locals call the "I-4 Eyesore."[1] It's a tall office building that can be seen for miles around. Sadly, it was to be the headquarters for a Christian television station, but both the funding and the energy for the project dried up, so now it stands unfinished. When I lived in Florida, I was embarrassed by the building because everyone knows it was being built by Christians, and Christians should have known better. You don't start a project like that unless you've counted the cost and are willing to work until the job is done.

Have you counted the cost of following Jesus, or does your life, like a towering eyesore, testify to the smallness of your faith?

Are you willing to give up anything and everything to reach someone for Jesus?

That's the thing about our faith: It can be quantified. We have either big faith or little faith (Luke 12:28).

How big is your faith?

Reaching lost people is going to require big faith and a huge investment of energy.

An Investment of Our Resources

It's also going to require a huge investment of our resources. Jesus compared being his disciple to a king preparing for battle against another king: "Won't he first sit down and consider whether he is able with ten thousand men to oppose the one coming against him with twenty thousand?" (Luke 14:31).

What resources do you have? Which are you willing to give up to reach lost people?

Are you willing to write a big check?

Are you willing to sell that old sports car that hasn't been driven for years?

Are you willing to let the church use your home as a small group location?

Are you willing to buy groceries for a needy family?

Are you willing to send money or supplies to an overseas missionary?

Are you willing to start giving at least 10 percent of your income to your church?

Are you willing to give up anything and everything to reach someone for Jesus? "Those of you who do not give up everything you have cannot be my disciples" (Luke 14:33). Give up everything?

But I thought that if I gave my life to Jesus, I was going to be healthy, wealthy, and wise. I thought following Jesus meant first-class seats, luxury cars, a gold watch, a spacious home in a gated community, perfect teeth, a silk suit, my "best life now," and the most important seats at the banquet.

I hate to break it to you, but that's not the picture Jesus painted. The picture Jesus painted looks an awful lot like a cross.

An Investment of Our Lives

"Whoever does not carry their cross and follow me cannot be my disciple" (Luke 14:27). A cross serves one purpose: to execute someone. A cross is not something you come off of alive. Jesus was saying that there are no uncrucified disciples. All disciples are supposed to be willing to sacrifice everything for Jesus. In the first century, many Christians did give up their lives for Jesus—and some did so on real crosses. Today, some Christians still die for their faith, but for most of us, carrying our cross means much less costly sacrifices like our energy and resources. Even so, Jesus' point is clear: If we are not willing to invest our lives in following him, we are not true disciples.

It's reported that nineteenth-century Danish philosopher Søren Kierkegaard said, "In the splendid cathedral, the high, well-born, highly honored, and worthy . . . Preacher, the chosen darling of the important people, steps before a select

Terry and Some Great Barbecue

I met Terry through a coworker shortly after I arrived in Kentucky. He was in his early forties and had zero church background. We began to eat lunch together on a regular basis. He wouldn't go to church, but he'd go to lunch with me. Over many lunches at the best barbecue places in our town, the barriers to his belief began to fall. Terry admitted that he was intrigued that he could eat with a preacher who seemed like a normal guy.

At the beginning of his journey, Terry was an agnostic—just looking for someone with whom to break bread. Now he breaks bread with his brothers and sisters in Christ as a believer, and interestingly, he has now adopted my approach and regularly eats lunch with his nonbelieving coworkers.

—MATT—

circle of the select, and *movingly* sermonizes on a text chosen by himself, namely, 'God has chosen the lowly and despised of the earth'—and no one laughs!"[2] Our self-indulgence is no laughing matter and solid evidence we've missed one of Jesus' clearest teachings. Jesus expects his followers to carry a cross.

My great-aunt Isabel Maxey got it. As a young woman, she felt God's call to take the gospel to Asia—Burma (now called Myanmar) in particular. She made many sacrifices to prepare for a life of service in this remote and dangerous country, not the least of which was to have all her teeth pulled because she didn't want anything as small as a toothache to distract her from the work. (Finding dental care on the field would be nearly out of the question.) She left family, friends, and the comforts of her life in the United States and began serving God in the jungles of Burma. During a home furlough, she fell in love with and married Warren Dittemore, and they returned to Burma together.

Their work was going well when Warren came down with typhoid fever. He died only seven months after arriving on the mission field. Aunt Isabel was left several thousand miles from home, alone with an infant daughter—but as far as she was concerned, nothing changed the fact that she had a calling to fulfill. So she and the new converts buried Uncle Warren's emaciated body and got back to work.

And that work almost cost her own life on several occasions. Shortly after Warren's death, Aunt Isabel had to escape with her daughter over the mountains just ahead of the Communists who were invading Burma. The Communist soldiers desecrated Warren's grave, hoping to dishearten the Christians in that village and stop the conversions to Christianity—but they failed. The number of Christians in that area grew steadily—and still grows to this day.

Aunt Isabel served forty years in Asia. God used her life and Uncle Warren's short life to reach countless people for Christ, because they chose to carry the cross of Christ. What amazing love and sacrifice!

Our comfort is not Jesus' priority. Dietrich Bonhoeffer said it this way: "When Christ calls a man, he bids him come and die."[3]

If we're looking for a comfortable faith, then we're not going to want to follow Jesus. If we're looking for a faith that won't cost us too much, then Christianity is not the right choice for us. It's time for you, me, and any others who call themselves Christian to put on our big boy and big girl pants, man up (and woman up too), pick up our crosses, and start investing our lives in our faith by inviting people to the great banquet.

Who's invited?

Your neighbors, the guy you cut off in traffic this morning, your boss, your ex-husband, your mother-in-law, the banker who denied your loan today, the renters who trashed your house, the single mom working at the gas station on the corner, and the women and children dying in Syria. There's room for everyone.

We invest our lives in so many things that don't matter. But we can begin now to invest in something that will not burn away.

An enthusiastic minister exhorted his congregation to

become more active in church affairs. "Brothers and sisters," he proclaimed, "what this church needs is the energy to get up and walk."

One of his deacons said, "Let her walk, brother, let her walk!"

The preacher raised his voice a little and added, "But we cannot be satisfied with walking; we've got to pick up speed and run."

The same deacon chimed in, "Let her run, my brother, let her run!"

The preacher was really getting into his message now. "But running's not enough either. One of these days this church has got to fly!"

That same deacon echoed, "Let her fly, brother, let her fly!"

The preacher paused for a moment and said solemnly, "But if this church is going to fly, we have to work harder and give more money—and sacrifice!"

The deacon said softly, "Let her walk, brother, let her walk."

I don't want the church to walk; I want the church to fly! I want lost people to be saved and—gladly—so does the church where I serve. We love to see lost people saved, so we love to give. This year, we've already given almost $300,000 away in cash and another $700,000 in assets to see lost people reached in Greeley and around the world. Our goal is to be giving away more than $1 million in cash every year by the year 2020.

We want the banquet hall to be full. So we will invest our energy, our resources, and our lives to that end.

I want Jesus' banquet hall to be full. So I will invest *my* energy, my resources, and my life to that end. And if you will join me, it will happen.

A young boy wanted to purchase a globe for his room. He found a store that had a globe he really liked that lit up from within. When he asked the clerk how much the globe cost, he was shocked to hear the price and exclaimed, "Wow! That's expensive."

And the clerk responded, "Yes, son, a lighted world costs more."

Yes, a lighted world costs more, but if you ask Jesus, he'll tell you it's well worth the investment.

INVESTING IN SOMETHING THAT REALLY MATTERS

- How much are you giving to your local church and world missions? Are you at 2 percent? 5 percent? Pledge now to increase your giving to the Lord and his work—in this country and internationally. Test the Lord with the tithe (10 percent). Step out in faith, start giving at least a tithe of your income, and see what God can do.

- How much time are you investing in the Lord's work? List one thing you can do this week that reflects a deeper commitment to the Lord's work.

12
JOY

"This son of mine was dead and is alive again; he was lost and is found." So they began to celebrate.

LUKE 15:24

What we celebrate says a lot about us.

Celebrating a wedding reveals your love of love. Celebrating a touchdown reveals your love of sports . . . and that you're not a Cleveland Browns fan! Celebrating a birth reveals that you love life. Celebrating an anniversary reveals that you love marriage. Celebrating an election reveals that you love politics. Celebrating Independence Day reveals that you love freedom. Celebrating a grand opening at Walmart reveals that you love bargains. Celebrating an A on your child's test reveals that you love learning, and celebrating Pigs in a Blanket Day reveals that you have no life!

What we celebrate reveals what we really love and who we really are. Jesus celebrated when lost people were found.

When I say lost people, which I know is not politically correct, I'm using the term the same way Jesus used it. I explained this in the introduction, but let me explain it here in more detail.

When I say someone is lost, I'm simply saying that the person is not where he or she is supposed to be.

When I say someone is lost, I'm simply saying that the person is not where he or she is supposed to be. Where are lost people supposed to be? Lost people are supposed to be with Jesus for all eternity. The sad thing is that so many lost people in this world have no idea they're lost. They are like the five-year-old boy I heard about who was with his parents at the mall. Somehow he and his parents got separated. His parents looked desperately for him but couldn't find him anywhere. Finally, a security guard found the boy. When the boy's parents arrived at the security desk, they found their son smiling and having a grand time, with a soft drink in his hands and his feet propped up on the desk. But when his parents called his name and he saw their faces, the boy started to cry. He didn't realize he was lost until he was found.

It's up to us to let lost people know that they are lost and that God wants them to be back where they're supposed to be.

And there are a lot of people who are not where they are supposed to be.

In their book *Lost in America*, Tom Clegg and Warren Bird point out that "within the next 24 hours, by our best estimates, several thousand people in the United States will die without knowing Jesus Christ and will spend an eternity separate from him as a result."[1]

That number makes me sad. Jesus came to this earth, lived a sinless life, died on a cross, and rose again so that every one of those lost people would have the chance to be back where they're supposed to be. It was his purpose—his obsession. As he said in Luke 19:10, "The Son of Man came to seek and to save the lost."

The Pharisees and teachers of the law didn't understand Jesus' passion for lost people. Luke 15:1 says it was the "tax collectors and sinners [who] were all gathering around to hear Jesus." Today it seems most "sinners" run from many Christians, but Jesus was different and they were attracted to him. They wanted to be around him because he wanted to be around them. They wanted to hear what he had to say because what he had to say gave them hope.

Lost people are just looking for hope. Some are looking for it in the pursuit of wealth, pleasure, relationships, corporate success, or physical perfection. Some look for hope in the emotional escape of intoxication or a drug-induced high.

Jesus gave sinners hope because he welcomed them, he accepted them, and he loved them. It wasn't an act; it wasn't to get a gold star or to check something off his spiritual to-do list. No, Jesus really loved lost people, so he accepted them, which had a strange effect on the Pharisees and teachers of the law. Luke wrote, "The Pharisees and the teachers of the law muttered, 'This man welcomes sinners and eats with them'" (Luke 15:2).

The word *mutter* is a sad word. Muttering is the opposite of joy. Muttering is what losers do. Muttering flows out of a bitter heart. Muttering is the native language of a sad soul.

Jesus gave sinners hope because he welcomed them, he accepted them, and he loved them.

Sometimes when we live in faithfulness to Jesus, it causes others to mutter—but we can't worry about their muttering. We must simply obey Jesus and move on. I hope that, like Jesus, I don't let anything keep me from finding as many lost people as possible and celebrating with joy each time. Jesus told three parables (Luke 15)—about a lost sheep, a lost coin, and a lost son—that illustrate his joy when lost people are found.

FINDING PEOPLE LOST BECAUSE OF THEIR OWN FOOLISHNESS = JOY

I've never been around sheep except for short visits to a petting zoo, but I hear that sheep are not very smart. Sheep are slaves to a herd mentality. Recently I read that fifteen hundred sheep in Turkey walked off a cliff one after another while their shepherds watched in horror. Sheep don't think very well for themselves, so a shepherd who has a sheep wander off knows that he must act quickly or the sheep may be killed.

People often don't think very well for themselves, either. I had to laugh when I read a few years ago about eleven people who lined up outside Grauman's Chinese Theater in Hollywood forty-six days before the premiere of *Star Wars:*

An Unplanned Party

I first met with Becky and her boyfriend, Todd, at Denny's to talk about church, but we ended up talking about Jesus, college, and the challenges of life. We met several times for lunch, and each time we grew to be better friends. Becky and Todd were interested in Jesus and taking greater steps to know him. As we talked, I sensed such happiness in their hearts and a longing for a deeper relationship with the Lord, so I wasn't surprised when they called to let me know that they wanted to be baptized the next Sunday.

Little did I know what a day of celebration that would be! Becky and Todd had been sharing the gospel with their friends, so when they showed up to be baptized, they came with a couple of friends and a cousin, who all wanted to be baptized too. It was a time of great joy and celebration as I baptized Becky, Todd, and the rest of the group into Jesus.

—SCOTT—

Episode III—Revenge of the Sith. One after another they took their places in line and set up their tents to begin the long wait for the premiere. Problem was, they were lining up at the wrong theater.[2]

In Jesus' first parable in Luke 15, a shepherd loses a sheep—or should we say a sheep loses his shepherd? With what we know about sheep, it seems safe to assume that the sheep in this story got lost because of his own foolishness. Maybe the sheep was captivated with a flower or too focused on nibbling a tuft of grass or distracted in some other way. Regardless, the sheep ended up not being where he was supposed to be. The shepherd then was so intent on finding the lost sheep that he left the ninety-nine other sheep in the open country to go and look for him.

Have you ever ended up lost due to a foolish choice?

Dewey did.

My sister and brother-in-law just moved to Boston. They rented a pod to pack their stuff. A day after getting the pod, their cat, Dewey, ran away. They searched and searched but couldn't find him. They finished packing, closed the pod, and it was shipped to a storage lot in Orlando where it sat for several days.

The pod was then shipped to Boston and arrived eleven days after it had been closed.

When my brother-in-law Shan opened the pod, he found that the couch had been destroyed. He immediately began searching the pod and found Dewey in a corner.

Dewey was skinny and shaken—but he was still alive.

Dewey just wandered away and refused to come back, and ended up trapped in a pod for eleven days.

Shan said that now Dewey will not leave his side. He follows him wherever he goes.

Can you relate to Dewey?

Ever wandered away from God and ignored his "calls" for you to come home?

I have.

Ever found yourself locked away in a "pod," feeling alone and forgotten?

I have.

Ever been delivered from that "pod" and been overcome with gratitude for being delivered?

I have, too.

If you can relate to that story, you understand why Dewey is sticking close to Shan.

When Shan found Dewey, he was so happy. He called my sister immediately to let her know her lost cat was found. Dewey was back where he was supposed to be. Shan didn't punish Dewey for making a bad choice. Of course not— Dewey is just a cat. No, this was not a time for punishment but for joyful celebration.

When the shepherd in Jesus' parable was reunited with his sheep, he didn't punish the sheep for making a bad choice, though it would not have been inappropriate. Sometimes a shepherd broke one leg of a sheep who wandered frequently, to keep the sheep closer to the shepherd. But not on this occasion with this sheep. No, this was a time for celebration, so the shepherd joyfully put the sheep on his shoulders.

But that's not all! This shepherd was so happy that he went home, called his friends and neighbors together, and said, "Rejoice with me; I have found my lost sheep" (Luke 15:6).

It's a sheep—not a beloved pet! Why was this shepherd so joyful?

The shepherd was joyful because he's not a shepherd—he's Jesus. And the sheep is not a sheep—it's us. Jesus doesn't care what we've done to find ourselves where we should not be. All he cares about is getting us back, and when he finds us, he throws a party.

FINDING PEOPLE LOST BECAUSE OF OUR NEGLECT = JOY

The next story Jesus tells in Luke 15 is about a woman who lost one of her ten silver coins. Each coin was worth about a day's wages. Though not a huge amount of money, most of us would be careful with a day's pay. So we get the sense that the coin was lost due in part to the neglect of the owner. Desperate to find her coin, the woman lit a lamp, swept the house, and searched. She moved everything in the house and, upon finding the coin, was so happy that she called her friends and neighbors together and said, "Rejoice with me; I have found my lost coin" (Luke 15:9).

Why was she so excited? It's a coin worth about sixteen cents, not a sheep or a beloved pet! Why was this woman so joyful?

She is Jesus, and the coin is us. Jesus desperately wants us back where we belong, and when he finds us, he throws a party.

A slew of people are spiritually lost, due in part to our neglect. We need to be more careful.

In Nazi Germany during World War II, there was a small group of Christian Germans who enjoyed their weekly worship. They enjoyed the preaching, the singing, and the fellowship . . . everything except the railroad track that brought noisy trains right behind the church. The noise was always distracting, but one Sunday it became disturbing. As the train passed by, the worshipers heard cries coming from the train. They eventually realized that these were the cries of Jews being carried away to concentration camps. Week after week the train whistle blew and the Christians heard the tracks rattle . . . and then the cries.

Disturbed by the screams, the Christians decided as a congregation that the only thing they could do was to sing hymns. They would sing so loud that they couldn't hear the cries of the desperate Jews being carried to their deaths. The cries were loud, but the hymns were louder.[3]

We must allow ourselves to hear the cries of the lost people in the world around us. George Barna

Jesus desperately wants us back where we belong, and when he finds us, he throws a party.

estimated there are between 180 and 190 million people in America who are not born-again Christians.[4] Can you get your mind around how many people that is?

- The New Orleans Superdome seats about 72,000 people. You could fill the Superdome 2,638 times with all the lost people in the United States.

- The combined population of Mexico and Ethiopia roughly equals the number of lost people in the United States.

- Imagine there's a huge fire coming toward this country and that everyone who wants to get out safely must come to you. If you could save 1,000 people a day, it would take you 521 years to save 190 million people.

Good news: You don't have to save 190 million people by yourself.

Bad news: There *is* a fire coming (2 Peter 3:7).

Good news: There is still time to help people get out safely.

Bad news: Too many Christians are doing absolutely nothing to reach anyone for Jesus.

Joy is a net of love by which you can catch souls.

—MOTHER TERESA

Good news: If you and I agree to stop neglecting lost people and we each find one lost person for Jesus next year, there would be two new Christians at the end of next year. If each of those formerly lost people finds another lost person in the next year, there would be four new Christians by the end of the next year. If this process continues, there would be eight new Christians by the end of the third year. If this process continues for the next forty years . . . 1,099,511,627,776 people will become Christians, which is roughly 163 times the current world population.

I say we do more than just sing. Let's allow ourselves to

hear the cries of lost people in need of salvation and get to work. We have some coins to find.

FINDING PEOPLE LOST BECAUSE OF THEIR OWN REBELLION = JOY

Jesus also teaches that some of the lost people who need to be returned to where they belong are not where they belong because they didn't want to be where they were supposed to be.

Did you ever run away? My brother-in-law did when he was a boy, but he only made it down to the Baptist church about four hundred yards away from his home in Elizabethton, Tennessee. He actually made it farther than the boy a police officer noticed walking around his block and carrying a suitcase. The boy circled the block twice, and finally the officer asked the boy what he was doing.

"I'm running away," the boy replied.

"But you keep walking in circles."

The boy answered, "That's because my mom told me I'm not allowed to cross the street without her permission."

I wish more people would choose to stay close to God instead of trying to run away from him, but too many of us are like the rebellious son in the last parable Jesus told in Luke 15.

It's a story about a father who had two sons. The older son was loyal, faithful, and good. His brother wanted the father dead. That's what it amounted to when this son asked for his inheritance while his father was still living.

Instead of being insulted, the father agreed to give his younger son his inheritance.

Now, as the younger son, he would receive only one-third of the family estate, while his older brother would inherit two-thirds. That was fine with him, so he took his portion and went off and squandered his wealth in wild living. When it was all gone and he was broke, this hungry young man turned to feeding pigs, the lowest work a Jew could do. Eventually, this wayward son came to his senses and headed for home with a repentant heart. He knew that he had sinned in rebelling against his father (Luke 15:18), and he was ready to be back home where he belonged—even if only as one of his father's hired hands.

While he was still far away, the father saw him, which tells us that his father had been watching for him all along. He was filled with compassion for his son, and the Bible says, "He ran to his son, threw his arms around him and kissed him" (Luke 15:20).

God runs.

Question: What makes us run?

Answer: Being late, catching a bus, fear, trying to lose weight.

Question: What makes God run?

Answer: Lost people.

The father was so overjoyed that he threw a party, which upset the older brother—but that's another story for another day. The father in this story was so joyful that he called his servants, friends, and neighbors together and said, "Let's have a feast and celebrate. For this son of mine was dead and is alive again; he was lost and is found" (Luke 15:23-24).

Why was he so excited? This time it's a little more obvious. He was filled with joy because his precious son was back where he belonged, and that's always cause for celebration. Jesus doesn't care that our own rebellion made us lost. All he cares about is getting us back, and when he finds us, he throws a party.

What we celebrate says a lot about us, which is why I celebrate every time a lost person is found and why I rejoice every time our passionate love for lost people makes some people mutter. If you read the rest of Jesus' story about the lost son, you'll see that the older brother missed out. Don't be that guy. Don't miss the party!

A person's conversion to Christ is always cause for celebration, and I'm very grateful that I've been able to witness, many times, the joy that comes when a lost person is back where he or she belongs.

I first met Phil at the local YMCA. He looked lonely, so I struck up a conversation with him. Honestly, he seemed like a lost sheep, and my heart was drawn to his condition. The more I got to know him, the more I realized that he was indeed lonely. I made it a point to work out at the same time he did so we could connect regularly. Eventually I arranged for us to meet for lunch at a local restaurant, which we did several times. Through our eating together we became good friends, and Phil began

Joy is the holy fire that keeps our purpose warm and our intelligence aglow.
—HELEN KELLER

to trust me. As I shared my faith with him, I could see him coming alive.

A few months after we first met, I had the privilege of baptizing Phil, surrounded by a crowd of Christians who cheered and applauded as he came up out of the water. It was pure joy. I'll never forget the look on his smiling face as he said, "They're clapping for me! It's like a party!"

MAKING BAPTISM A TIME FOR CELEBRATION

- Applause is a very appropriate response to someone's baptism, so feel free to clap—along with all of heaven (Luke 15:7)—after someone finds his or her way back to God.

- Singing a song before and/or after the baptism can make the time of conversion a time of worship as well as celebration.

- Video each baptism. At the end of the year, combine these into one, set it to music, and show it during a service in order to celebrate what God has done in the lives of people in your church.

13

VISION

When Jesus reached the spot, he looked up.

LUKE 19:5

There are many kinds of vision problems. Myopia, nearsightedness. Hypermetropia, farsightedness. Amblyopia, lazy eye. Heterotropia, crossed eyes.

There's also I-say-I'm-a-Christian-but-I-don't-see-like-Jesus-did-opia, not seeing lost people as Jesus did.

Jesus didn't have any vision problems. He saw lost people. They weren't invisible to him. He didn't rush by them. He didn't ignore them. He wasn't too busy for them.

He saw them crying by themselves on the back row of the church.

He saw them dropping off their kids at day care so they could make it to their second job.

He saw them standing with a Scotch in hand and looking overwhelmed at the class reunion.

He didn't step to the right side of the sidewalk when he saw them standing on the left. He didn't make assumptions about them because of the way they dressed. He didn't avoid being seen with them because of how that might affect his ministry.

He didn't look at lost people as if they were second-class citizens. He didn't see their tattoos and piercings as obstacles to their salvation. He didn't see their "Will work for food" sign and think cynically, *Yeah, right.* He didn't see their addictions as disqualifiers that needed to be conquered before they could come back to church.

He didn't see them as sin, but sinners who needed salvation.

He didn't see lost people as lost causes, because—to Jesus—there are no lost causes! Jesus loves lost people, so he saw them.

In August 1985, a group of lifeguards were having a pool party to celebrate their first drowning-free swimming season ever. Four on-duty lifeguards watched over the party as well, but as the party ended, everyone was surprised to find the body of Jerome Moody at the bottom of the deep end of the pool. No one had seen him drown.[1]

Jesus saw people.

Once you start looking in the Bible for Christ's vision for lost people, it's like shopping for a red Subaru. Have you ever stopped in to check out a red Subaru at a dealership, decided to think about it overnight, and then saw red Subarus

To Jesus—there are no lost causes!

everywhere while driving home? They were there all along, but you didn't notice them until you started thinking about red Subarus.

Once we start thinking about lost people, we'll start seeing them everywhere, like Jesus did.

- When Jesus *saw her*, he called her forward and said to her, "Woman, you are set free from your infirmity" (Luke 13:12, emphasis added in all these verses).

- When Jesus *saw him* lying there and learned that he had been in this condition for a long time, he asked him, "Do you want to get well?" (John 5:6).

- When Jesus *saw her* weeping, and the Jews who had come along with her also weeping, he was deeply moved in spirit and troubled (John 11:33).

- Jesus *looked at him* and loved him (Mark 10:21).

- When Jesus reached the spot, he *looked up* and said to him, "Zacchaeus, come down immediately. I must stay at your house today" (Luke 19:5).

Jesus saw Zacchaeus, which is a little surprising, because at first glance Jesus seeing Zacchaeus doesn't seem to be the point of this story (Luke 19:1-10). The first four verses of this passage introduce us to a short man who was working really hard to see Jesus. We aren't told why he wanted to see Jesus, or that he was a believer in Jesus, or that he was interested in becoming a believer of Jesus; we're just told that he wanted to see Jesus.

I remember wanting to see President Bill Clinton.

A tornado hit a trailer park across the street from a college where I worked in central Florida. About a dozen people were killed. It was terrible. At the end of the week, President Clinton came to the trailer park to make a speech about how much he cared and how the government was going to help the people impacted by the storm to get back on their feet. I remember wanting to see the president up close, so I worked really hard to maneuver myself through the crowd into a position where I could see him walk by. I wasn't a fan of his; still, I wanted to see him for myself. It's not every day you get to see the president up close.

Seeing him was kind of a letdown. He looked more normal and wrinkly than I expected.

Maybe it was the same thing with Jesus for Zacchaeus. Maybe he didn't really like Jesus or prefer his politics. Maybe he just wanted to see him up close. It's not every day you get to see a man who claims to be your Messiah, so, like me with President Clinton, Zacchaeus worked hard to position himself where he could see Jesus.

I respect Zacchaeus. He wasn't going to let anything keep him from seeing Jesus, including the crowd or his lack of height, so he climbed a sycamore-fig tree to get a better view. Sycamore-fig trees could be thirty to forty feet tall, with short trunks and plenty of branches that were easily accessible from the ground.

I respect Jesus. He's wonderful. He was intent on seeing Zacchaeus. He wasn't going to let anything keep him from seeing Zacchaeus, including the crowd or Zacchaeus's lack of height.

Isn't that interesting? We always focus on how intent Zacchaeus was on seeing Jesus, but have you thought about how intent Jesus was on seeing Zacchaeus?

We all need to know how much Jesus wants to see us—and see us saved.

There were a ton of people in Jericho who wanted to see Jesus. Have you ever tried to find someone in a large crowd? It's much easier to find someone in a large crowd these days because of cell phones, but Jesus didn't have this option. Well, I guess he could have invented a cell phone for himself and Zacchaeus if he so desired, but then he would have had to invent plastic, cell phone towers, electricity, satellites, microchips, malls, cell phone kiosks, customer service agents who aren't very helpful, and a million ringtones of the latest Top 40 hits being sung by the youth in Jerusalem. That would have been a little complicated, so he just found "the spot" and looked up.

That's what the text says: "When Jesus reached the spot, he looked up" (Luke 19:5).

That's the first key to seeing people as Jesus saw people.

SEEING PEOPLE . . . WHERE THEY ARE

Where are lost people? Everywhere. They work with you, play with you, and maybe even live with you. They're sitting next to you in biology class, coaching your daughter's soccer team, complaining that you don't come home for Christmas anymore, married to your ex-husband, sitting in the seat at church in front of you and in the sycamore-fig tree next to the road.

Jesus met Zacchaeus where he was. He met him at "the spot." What is the spot? It's the place where grace and sin meet—and where hope is born. Jesus didn't expect Zacchaeus to meet him at his spot, because Jesus didn't have a spot. Jesus said it this way: "Foxes have dens and birds have nests, but the Son of Man has no place to lay his head" (Luke 9:58). Sometimes it appears we have it wrong when we expect sinners to meet us at our spot. The outreach programs of most churches seem to be built around the goal of getting lost people to come to church (our spot), which I admit can be very effective. But I'd love to see more programs that effectively get Christians to go meet lost people at their spots.

I look upon all the world as my parish.

—JOHN WESLEY

In this event we see Jesus meeting Zacchaeus at his spot. In the previous chapter, we learned that Jesus wants us to leave the ninety-nine sheep in the open field and go out to search for the one lost sheep. He wants us to move the furniture and search the entire house for the lost coin. He wants us to run out and meet the lost son as he's making a turn for home. He wants us to "go and make disciples of all nations" (Matthew 28:19). He wants our spot to be wherever lost people are.

Jesus didn't expect Zacchaeus to find him. He didn't send Zacchaeus a home mailer with directions to his spot. He didn't put a map in the Yellow Pages showing him ten different ways to get to his spot. He didn't hang a banner with the words "Come Worship at Our Spot!" on his church building. No, Jesus didn't expect Zacchaeus to do all the work, so he met him where he was.

People want to know that their existence matters. They want to know they matter.

Fish don't jump into the boat. Good soil doesn't jump onto the seeds. Disciples don't make themselves. Sheep, coins, and sons don't find themselves. We have to go to their spots and look for them.

Jesus went to the spot where he knew he could find Zacchaeus, and when he arrived there, he looked at him.

Lost people want to be seen.

I think that's why so many teens work so hard to make their physical appearance as shocking as humanly possible. They want people to see them—to notice them. Critical attention is better than no attention at all.

I think that's why so many men invest so much time and energy in achieving visible success in the business world, or in having the nicest yard on the block or the nicest car in the parking garage. They want people to see them—to notice them.

I think that's why so many women seem obsessed with enhancing, preserving, restoring, and revealing their bodies.

People want to know that their existence matters. They want to know they matter. Jesus looked up and saw Zacchaeus because Zacchaeus mattered to Jesus.

Jesus then did the next most important thing we can do in the same situation: He spoke to Zacchaeus. He said, "Zacchaeus, come down immediately. I must stay at your house today" (Luke 19:5). Jesus could see where Zacchaeus was—up a tree—and knew that he was not where he was supposed to be, so he invited himself to his house. Zacchaeus accepted the offer immediately and happily.

Why?

Do you know what I would have done if President Clinton had stopped in front of me, looked me in the eye, and said, "Arron, come out here immediately. I must stay at your house today"? I would have said, "Fantastic!"

Zacchaeus was just hoping for a glimpse of Jesus, and now Jesus was declaring to the entire crowd that he had selected him to be his host for the day. This was a big deal. Jesus hadn't waited for Zacchaeus to invite him; he skipped that step altogether, inviting himself to Zacchaeus's house and proclaiming to the crowd that Zacchaeus mattered.

People just want to matter. Legalists just want to mutter.

Luke wrote, "All the people saw this and began to mutter, 'He has gone to be the guest of a sinner'" (Luke 19:7). At least legalists are consistent. You always know what you're going to get from them.

SEEING PEOPLE . . . AND WHAT THEY CAN BE

The crowd of people saw Zacchaeus only as a sinner. That's not who Jesus saw. Jesus saw a lost man who needed to be found. Through being seen this way, Zacchaeus saw the need to change and was transformed in several important ways, as Luke 19:8 tells us.

First, Zacchaeus "stood up." What does that mean? Was Zacchaeus sitting? Or is this Luke's way of telling us that Zacchaeus had been immediately transformed into a man of great stature—morally speaking? I choose to believe the latter.

Second, Zacchaeus said, "Look, Lord!" He was no longer a man desperate for a glimpse of a celebrity but a man who had seen the face of his Lord.

And third, Zacchaeus, a chief tax collector who stole money from his fellow Jews on behalf of the Roman government, promised to give half of his possessions to the poor and repay four times the amount of money he had obtained dishonestly.

Being seen for who you can be is a powerful and transformational force.

Cheryl grew up in the country and used to hang out at her father's small grocery store. When Cheryl was only four years old, the milkman who delivered milk to her father's store would come into the store and greet her with, "How's my little Miss America?" At first, little Cheryl just giggled at this friendly milk-man, but eventually she became comfortable with his greeting. She began to look forward to the milkman's arrival and liked his "Miss America" question. As she grew, the milkman's words of a child's fantasy transformed into a teenager's dream and, finally, into an achievable goal. In 1980, Cheryl

Jesus showed everyone that he sees lost people not as distractions but as his purpose for being on this planet.

Prewitt stood on a stage in Atlantic City and was crowned Miss America as the nation watched![2]

That milkman changed Cheryl's life. We can do the same thing by simply seeing people for who they can be.

Jesus wasn't shortsighted when it came to Zacchaeus. He saw Zacchaeus as a man with potential who needed salvation and needed to be welcomed gladly by his own people, so he proclaimed for all to hear: "Today salvation has come to this house, because this man, too, is a son of Abraham. For the Son of Man came to seek and to save the lost" (Luke 19:9-10).

We are limited, not by our abilities, but by our vision.
—UNKNOWN

Jesus showed the people of Jericho that he saw Zacchaeus not as a man who had fallen short and needed to be punished, but as a man who was now saved. By calling Zacchaeus a son of Abraham, Jesus showed that he saw Zacchaeus as truly repentant and worthy to be honored among his own, which is important because, as R. C. Foster noted, "Publicans [tax collectors] were regarded as having forfeited their birthright as sons of Abraham."[3]

In reminding us that he was at this spot to seek and save what was lost, Jesus showed everyone that he saw lost people not as distractions but as his purpose for being on this planet.

What do you see when you look at lost people?

When Yukio Shige sees lost people, he sees people who need to be saved, as a *Time* magazine article reveals.

Shige sees lost people at the Tojinbo cliffs in Japan almost every day. He knows they're lost, because they aren't looking at the view. "They don't carry a camera or souvenir gifts," he said in the article. "They don't have anything. They hang their heads and stare at the ground."[4]

When Shige sees these lost souls, he approaches them with a smile and a simple hello. He might ask them about how they came to the cliffs and where they're staying, and—if given the chance—he might lightly touch one shoulder. When he does this, Shige says, the person he's talking to often breaks into tears. These people, the lost souls who come to the Tojinbo cliffs with no camera and no souvenirs, have not come to see the view; they've come to end their lives.

The Tojinbo cliffs are a well-known site for suicide. Shige, a retired detective, knows this, so two or three times a day he patrols the cliffs, trying to prevent lost souls from taking their lives. If he can talk them off the cliffs, he invites them back to his office and eats with them.

The *Time* article details these important meals: "There's no rush in Shige's office. He offers those who go there oroshi-mochi, a dish of pounded sticky rice served with grated radish. Traditionally the food is prepared to celebrate the New Year, with each family taking its own rice to be mixed with that of its neighbors. 'When people come here and eat mochi, they remember their childhood—father, mother, siblings, hometown. They remember they're not alone,' Shige says."[5]

These meals are working. Shige has prevented 188 people from committing suicide. He's literally saved 188 lives!

The article notes that the melody of "Amazing Grace" plays when Shige's cell phone rings. Now I have to admit the obvious: A religious ringtone doesn't mean Shige's a Christian, especially since "Amazing Grace" is known in Japan even

Happy Hour

I have been a Christian all my life. I was baptized when I was six, I'm a graduate of a Bible college, and I've been a small group leader for many years. I met Sam through a small group I led. She lived a few houses down the street. We got to know each other through a meeting I hosted called Happy Hour.

Happy Hour was an idea from a friend in Seattle. It seemed like a great way to mix my newest hobby—home beer brewing—with my passion for reaching people for Jesus. Happy Hour is a low-key cross between a cocktail party and a weekly small group, where we discussed everything from work to school to church to the beer we were drinking.

Sam came to Happy Hour regularly and got to know many of my other friends, most of whom are Christians. Sam was searching for something more for her life. She grew up going to church and went to a Christian high school, and I think her mom is a pastor or minister of some kind back in Seattle. But since coming to our town, Sam had more or less given up on all that and moved into a house with her boyfriend.

Well, Sam spent a lot of time with us at Happy Hour, and eventually— through the relationships she developed with us—she found her way back to church and out of her boyfriend's house. It made us happy that it all came about because we invited her to join us for Happy Hour.

—DAVID—

among the general population. I can't prove whether Shige is a Christian or not, but I think I can prove—based on his actions—that Shige loves helping people who are lost in this life.

The *Time* article ends with this quote from Shige: "I want Tojinbo to be the most challenging place. Not where life ends, but where it begins."[6]

I pray that you'll see people who are not where they are supposed to be, go to their "spot," look at them, and simply say, "How about you and I get something to eat?"

I pray that you'll join me in eating with sinners and in making our dinner tables the most challenging places—not where life ends, but where it begins.

SEEING LOST PEOPLE

- Practice looking at people and assuming the best, not the worst. A local mall is a good place to try this out.

- Develop the habit of praying for the people you see daily. You will find that this practice helps you to see people the way Jesus does.

Acknowledgments

The title for this book came from a T-shirt that Michael Altman created many years ago. Mike, thanks for using your talents for God's glory, for creating a shirt that God has used—while I was wearing it—to start meaningful conversations with non-Christians, and for allowing me to use *Eats with Sinners* as the title of this book. I'm so grateful, my friend.

To Rhonda, my wife—thank you for being patient and supportive throughout our marriage and while I was writing this book. I adore you. How do you keep your wings and halo hidden? Loves.

To my children: Ashton and CJ Jenkins, Levi, Sylas, Payton—my precious ones. I'm grateful for every meal we share around our table at home. It's heaven to me. I pray that each of you will make it your purpose to go to heaven and take as many people with you as possible. RWYA!

My family: Mom, the Chamberses, the Holbrooks, the Woods, and the Smiths—I love you all.

My agent, Blythe Daniel—you are the best! I love serving with you. I wouldn't want to do this without you.

My publishing team at NavPress: Don Pape, Caitlyn Carlson, Melissa Myers, Stephanie Wright, and David Zimmerman—I really love how you guys love Jesus!

Dale Reeves, thanks for believing in this book before it was even a book.

My manuscript editor for the first edition, Diane Stortz—your keen insights, biblical knowledge, and spiritual sensitivities blessed the words of this book—and me—beyond words. Thanks!

Twila Sias, thanks for all you did to help me finish this book. I love you.

My covenant group: Alan Ahlgrim, Rick Grover, Greg Marksberry, Bryan Myers.

My friends: the Davises; the Estrins; the Fasts; the Floreses; Frontier Academy cross-country, track, and basketball teams; Cash Hunter; Travis Jacob; Steve Jackson; my assistant, Stephany Jenkins; Caleb Kaltenbach; the Lewises; the Lightfeet; the Longs; Isaiah Magana; Andrew Peterson and *The War of Art*; John Plastow; Ross Runnels; Leanne Schaffner; Brett Shanklin; the Streets; Brad Warren; Darlene Schroeder; the late Delmar Schroeder; the staff and elders of Journey Christian Church; and my church family—I'm still enjoying the journey!

My readers—I'm so grateful for each of you. I pray this book fills you with a hunger to eat with a bunch of sinners. Blessings!

For Reflection and Discussion

CHAPTER 1: INTEGRITY

For Personal Study and Reflection: Write the name of a Christian you think is a person of integrity. List three adjectives that describe this person and prove he or she is a person of integrity.

For Group Study and Discussion: Ask group members to each bring a photo of someone they believe to be a person of integrity. As the group time begins, have people show their photos and tell why they believe the person in the photo has integrity.

1. Who first introduced you to Jesus Christ? Describe what happened.

2. As you reflect on your conversion and how God used this person to introduce you to Jesus, which of the following had the biggest impact: what the person said to you, how the person lived, or some other factor?

3. Describe a time when God gave you a chance to share your faith. What were your three biggest concerns during this evangelistic experience?

4. Read Luke 4:1-13. Jesus was hungry, and then Satan tempted him to turn some stones into bread (Luke 4:3). What does this teach us about Satan? What can we do to prepare ourselves for attacks like this?

5. Satan showed Jesus all the kingdoms of the world and then offered them all to Jesus (Luke 4:5-7). Understanding that Satan doesn't own anything, what does this temptation teach us about him?

6. The devil quoted Scripture to Jesus (Luke 4:10-11). What does this reveal about Satan?

7. Jesus rebutted Satan's attacks by quoting Scripture (Luke 4:4, 8, 12). What can we learn from this example about the power of God's Word to help when we are being attacked by the devil? What is one thing you can do this week to learn more Scripture?

8. What would have happened to Jesus' ministry if he had given in to any of these three temptations?

9. We are all sinners (Romans 3:23) who will, at one time or another, experience a moral failure of some type. How does a moral failure that has not been dealt with affect our efforts to share our faith with lost friends? On the other hand, how does a moral failure that has been dealt with help us as we share our faith?

10. What did this time of testing reveal about Jesus' character? How did this time of testing prepare him for his ministry to lost people? How have your times of spiritual testing prepared you to be a better evangelist?

This week I will set up a meal with _____ to focus on building a relationship through which I can introduce my friend to Jesus.

CHAPTER 2: ACCESSIBILITY

For Personal Study and Reflection: Find a box, a marker, and a box cutter. Take a few moments to reflect on the similarities between a church building and a box. On the outside of the box, write these similarities. Now take a few moments to reflect on what we can do to make the gospel more accessible. On the inside of the box, write these strategies. Then carefully cut the box open and flatten it so that the outreach strategies are exposed. Reflect on what you can do to make the gospel more accessible to lost people.

For Group Study and Discussion: Adapt the above idea for your group. Place the box in the center of the group and discuss the similarities and strategies together. Pray for each thing that your church can do to make the gospel more accessible to lost people.

1. Have you ever accidentally locked yourself out of your home, office, or car? Describe what you did to gain access. How did you feel while you were locked out? What did you learn from this experience?

2. This chapter identifies two physical barriers that Christians can put between lost people and the hope of salvation. Can you think of any others? What are they?

3. List three of the biggest spiritual barriers that Christians put between lost people and the hope of salvation.

4. Read Luke 4:14-15, 31-32, 38; 6:17-19; 7:11; 10:1; John 3:16. According to these verses, where are some of the places that Jesus went to share the gospel? What do these verses teach us about what Jesus was willing to do to make the gospel accessible to lost people?

5. What is one thing you can do to make the gospel more accessible to lost people?

6. What is one thing our church can do to make the gospel more accessible?

This week I will set up a meal with _____ to focus on building a relationship through which I can introduce my friend to Jesus. During our meal I will ask my friend to share a few of the things that he or she doesn't like about most churches. I will not get defensive or try to fix the problem; I will simply listen, seeking understanding.

CHAPTER 3: GRACE

For Personal Study and Reflection: What is the meanest thing you've ever heard a Christian say? The nicest thing? Reflect on how each statement might be received by a lost person.

For Group Study and Discussion: Ask group members to bring clippings from magazines, newspapers, and Internet news reports that reflect the world's opinion of Christians and the church. Suggest that they search the phrase "What do you think of Christians?" online. To begin your session, discuss the relevance of these opinions in light of your group members' experiences. Is the world's opinion of Christians and the church fair? Why or why not?

1. Recall a time when someone was mean to you. What did you learn about life from that experience? What did you learn about yourself? Without naming names, what did you learn about others?

2. Note a time when someone was exceptionally nice to you. What did you learn about life from that experience? What did you learn about yourself? What did you learn about others?

3. Read Luke 4:16-30. In this account, Jesus read a passage from Isaiah, and all who heard him were amazed at the "gracious words" he spoke. Have you ever heard a Christian leader speak "gracious words"? What was the impact of that leader's message on your life?

4. Jesus' audience tried to kill him because he reminded them that God had come to bring help and healing to all people—not just the Israelites. Have you ever heard a message from a preacher or teacher that was completely true but still upset you? What was your response? Why?

5. Do you think most Christians would rather hear a message that steps on their toes or one that makes them feel good about themselves? Why? What about non-Christians?

6. Individually and as a group, what are some practical things you can do to bring:
   - good news to the poor?
   - freedom for the prisoners?
   - sight for the blind?
   - release for the oppressed?

7. As we share the gospel with lost people, what are three things we need to remember so that we'll share the message in a gracious way?

This week I will set up a meal with _____ to start building a relationship through which I can introduce this friend to Jesus. During our meal I will focus on speaking gracious words.

CHAPTER 4: FAITH

For Personal Study and Reflection: Reflect on a time when you had to do something that required a lot of faith. What did you learn from that experience? If you could make any one of your dreams a reality today, which one would it be? Why? What step of faith can you take today to make this dream a reality?

For Group Study and Discussion: Ask members to share testimonies of times they had to take a step of faith. Discuss what each member learned from his or her experience.

1. When you hear the word *faith*, what is the first image to pop into your mind? Why?

2. In Hebrews 11 we read what is often referred to as the roll call of the faithful. If you were listing the names of all the faithful people you know (not in the Bible), what three people would be at the top of your list? Why?

3. Read Luke 5:1-11. Have you ever been fishing? What do you like best about fishing? What do you like least?

4. Did you catch anything while fishing? What did you catch and how did you catch it? What was the most effective bait you used in each situation?

5. What things guarantee success in both fishing and faith? Explain.

6. Jesus told Simon Peter to "put out into deep water, and let down the nets for a catch" (Luke 5:4). As you think about the next year, what deep-water event or experience do you foresee will require you to let down your nets in faith? What is one thing you can do this week to prepare for this act of faith?

7. Simon Peter thought catching more fish was a lost cause, but Jesus helped him and the other fishermen realize that with Jesus there are no lost causes. Write the first name of a lost person you know who might be considered a lost cause. Pray and ask God to help you to reach him or her for Jesus Christ.

This week I will set up a meal with _____ (a "lost cause") to begin or continue building a relationship through which I can introduce my friend to Jesus. During our meal, I will focus on helping this person to know that with Jesus there is always hope.

CHAPTER 5: INTIMACY

For Personal Study and Reflection: List the names of as many of your neighbors as you can. Then beside each name write one thing you know about that neighbor. How do you feel about your relationships with your neighbors?

For Group Study and Discussion: Ask group members to each do the above activity. Go over the lists together and reflect on what they reveal.

1. With whom (besides a spouse) do you have an intimate relationship? What makes your relationship intimate? What are your favorite aspects of this relationship? How much time did it take before the relationship reached the level it is today?

2. What are some of the blessings of intimate relationships? What are some of the risks of intimate relationships?

3. Read Luke 5:27-32. Levi was a tax collector. What type of person today would you say is most like the tax collectors in Jesus' day? Why?

4. Why do you think Levi was so willing to leave everything and follow Jesus immediately? Would you have been willing to do the same thing?

5. Describe the biggest party you've ever been to. What was your favorite part of that experience? Why do you think Levi threw a party for Jesus and his tax-collector friends? If you were to throw a similar party, what are some of the things you'd do to make it a blessing to your non-Christian friends?

6. Individually or as a group, plan to host a party for some non-Christian friends. Jot down a couple of ideas. Set a date for this party in the near future.

This week I will set up a meal with _____ to establish or build a relationship through which I can introduce my friend to Jesus. During our meal, I will focus on developing more intimacy in our relationship.

CHAPTER 6: TOLERANCE

For Personal Study and Reflection: Get on your computer and search the word *tolerance*. List the top three words that come to mind as you read some of the Web pages that are brought up during your search.

For Group Study and Discussion: Say the word *tolerance* and ask group members to share the first words that pop into their minds. Then say *intolerance* and ask the same question. Did anyone think of Christians when one of those words was mentioned? Which word? Why?

1. Who is the most famous person you've heard of who embodies the word *tolerant*? Why? Who is the most

famous person you've heard of who embodies the word *intolerant*? Why? Which of these people do you most relate to? Why?

2. Let's be honest here. What kind of person do you find difficult to tolerate? Why?

3. Read Luke 7:36-50. Have you ever paid off a huge debt? What kind of sacrifices did you make to pay off the debt? How long did it take? How did you feel when the debt was finally paid off?

4. How tolerant are you of yourself when you're in debt? If you were a lender, would you find it hard to be tolerant of your borrowers? Why or why not?

5. Have you ever had a financial debt canceled by a lender? Did that experience make you more willing to go into debt, or did it make you more committed to stay out of debt? Why? How did that make you feel about your lender?

6. What spiritual debts has Jesus canceled—paid off— for you? How should that affect how tolerant you are toward lost people?

This week I will set up a meal with _____ to help me build a relationship through which I can introduce my friend to Jesus. During our meal, I will focus on being tolerant of my non-Christian friend.

CHAPTER 7: RESOLVE

For Personal Study and Reflection: List your top three goals for the next year. Beside each goal write one thing you'll have to do to make that goal a reality.

For Group Study and Discussion: Ask group members to list the top three goals they have for the next year. Then ask them to share why these goals are important to them and what they are willing to do to accomplish their goals.

1. Name one of your greatest accomplishments. What sacrifices did you have to make in order to attain that goal?

2. Name one of your greatest failures. What did you learn from the experience?

3. What are two of your biggest motivators? Why do these things motivate you?

4. Read Luke 9:51-56. What motivated Jesus? Why?

5. In this passage, what seems to be motivating James and John? Can you relate? Recall a time when you felt like calling fire down on someone. What did you learn from that experience that has helped you to be a better Christian today?

6. List one thing you are resolved to do for Jesus in the next year. What is one thing that you know you will have to do in order to reach that goal?

7. List the names of three people you'd like to reach for Jesus. Beside each name list one thing you're going to do to help bring them to Jesus.

This week I will set up a meal with _____ to focus on building a relationship through which I can introduce my friend to Jesus. Before our meal I will carefully consider my goal for this relationship. During the meal, I will let that goal guide what I say and how I listen.

CHAPTER 8: URGENCY

For Personal Study and Reflection: Set the alarm on your watch (or timer) for thirty seconds. Press start, and before the alarm sounds, write the names of as many lost people as you can plus something notable about each of them. Then take some time to pray for every person on your list.

For Group Study and Discussion: Adapt the above activity for your group. Before prayer time, ask the group to reflect on how they did and how that felt.

1. How many days a week do alarms dictate what you do? List the types of alarms you hear regularly.

2. Describe your busiest day in the past week. Were you able to get everything done? If so, how? How often do you have days like that?

3. Have you ever been to, worked on, or lived on a farm? What was the best part of that experience? Worst part? What lessons did you learn?

4. Read Luke 10:1-24. Why do you think Jesus used the harvest image as a picture of evangelism? What lessons should we learn from his use of that image?

5. What qualities must a worker have in order to do a good job bringing in Jesus' harvest? Do you believe you have those qualities? Why or why not?

6. What is one thing you can do this week to help Jesus bring in the harvest?

7. Pray for every person on your list. Set the alarm for thirty seconds again and let it go off during your prayer as a reminder that we have much work to do before Jesus returns.

This week I will set up a meal with _____ to focus on building a relationship through which I can introduce my friend to Jesus. During our meal, I will look for opportunities to talk about the important and timely issues that might be keeping my friend from committing to Christ.

CHAPTER 9: MERCY

For Personal Study and Reflection: Which of your favorite movies has the best story of revenge? Watch that movie and think about the story of the Good Samaritan. Compare and contrast what you see in the movie with the story of the Good Samaritan.

For Group Study and Discussion: Show a few well-known movie scenes that depict people taking revenge or being recipients of vengeful acts (*Star Wars, The Wizard of Oz, The Princess Bride*, for example). Let group members discuss how these scenes make them feel, and why.

1. When have you had an opportunity to take revenge on someone? What thoughts go through your mind in a situation like that?

2. When has someone had mercy on you? What did you learn from that situation?

3. Read this old German proverb and react: "Revenge converts a little right into a great wrong." Do you have any personal experience to validate this claim? Explain.

4. Read Luke 10:25-37. (If you're in a group that is up for it, act out this parable. Have one person read the biblical account while the characters act out the scenes.) Which character do you relate to most in this story? Why?

5. The priest and the Levite passed by the wounded man. What are some reasons we use as justification for "passing by" the spiritually, physically, and emotionally wounded people in our world?

6. Name someone who has been a Good Samaritan to you. In what way?

7. How can you be a better neighbor to the people in your world this week? Be specific.

This week I will set up a meal with _____ to focus on building a relationship through which I can introduce my friend to Jesus. During our meal, I will concentrate on speaking words of mercy into our relationship.

CHAPTER 10: HUMILITY

For Personal Study and Reflection: Write the name of the most arrogant person you know, followed by the name of the humblest person you know. Reflect on the differences between the two people. Then pray this prayer: "God, please keep me humble, even when the world gives me much attention. Free me of any pride that would keep me from doing your will."

For Group Study and Discussion: Ask group members to name song titles (country music or otherwise) that best describe their lives right now and to explain why. Then ask what song titles they would like to describe their lives in the coming year.

1. Who is the humblest person you know? Why do you think this person is humble? Do you think it's easy for this person to be humble, or do you think he or she has to work at it?

2. What is something that you're really good at? Is it hard for you to be humble while participating in this activity?

3. What are some of the factors in life that make it hard for us to be humble? What can we do as Christians to humble ourselves?

4. Read Luke 14:1-14. Have you ever had dinner with a famous or "important" person? What was that experience like?

5. When you were growing up, who sat where at your dinner table? Did you like your seat?

6. What was your best birthday party? What made the party so special? Who was invited?

7. Jesus taught that when we give a banquet, we need to invite the poor, the crippled, the lame, and the blind. Individually or as a group, list people you could invite to a party—people who are outside the circle of those you might normally invite. Pray that God will open a door of opportunity for you to invite these people to a party and give you the courage to walk through the door when it opens.

This week I will set up a meal with _____ to focus on building a relationship through which I can introduce my friend to Jesus. During our meal, I will keep a humble attitude.

CHAPTER 11: INVESTMENT

For Personal Study and Reflection: Choose a room in your home and look around at all the stuff in it. Estimate how much each item is worth and note the total. How does this make you feel? Of all the things in the room, which item do you value most? Why?

What is the most valuable item you possess? Why?

List the names of some people who are important to you. Beside each name list a word that helps to describe why this person is so valuable to you.

For Group Study and Discussion: In advance, ask group members to bring with them an item they value. Start your session by allowing each person to explain the value this item has to him or her.

1. What is the worst purchase you've ever made? What did you learn from that experience?

2. What is the best investment you've ever made? What did you learn from that experience?

3. What is the best financial advice you've ever been given? Have you followed it? Why or why not?

4. Read Luke 14:25-35. In this passage Jesus says, "If anyone comes to me and does not hate father and mother, wife and children, brothers and sisters—yes, even their own life—such a person cannot be my disciple" (verse 26). What does this mean? Do you

know of anyone like Isabel and Warren Dittemore, who had to pay a high price for following Jesus?

5. Jesus also said, "Whoever does not carry their cross and follow me cannot be my disciple" (Luke 14:27). When you think about the cross, what images come to mind? When your non-Christian friends think about the cross, what do you think comes to their minds?

6. What does it mean to carry our crosses today?

7. In Luke 14:33, Jesus said, "Those of you who do not give up everything you have cannot be my disciples." Name one thing you've given up for Jesus. What else might you give up for him in the coming year?

8. Write the first name of a person you know who is not a Christian but for whom you're willing to invest so that he or she can know more about Jesus' love. Ask God to make it clear what you must be willing to sacrifice in order to reach this person with the gospel.

This week I will set up a meal with _____ to focus on building a relationship through which I can introduce my friend to Jesus. During our meal, I will look for clues about ways to invest more of myself in reaching my friend with the gospel.

CHAPTER 12: JOY

For Personal Study and Reflection: Get out a photo album (could be on your computer) and find pictures of yourself experiencing joy. What was the occasion, and why were you feeling joyful? Reflect on what these pictures teach you about joy.

For Group Study and Discussion: Ask group members to bring pictures of themselves that express joy. Let each person explain why he or she was feeling joyful in the picture.

1. Describe a time in your life when you experienced true joy. Why did this experience make you joyful?

2. Have you ever experienced the joy of finding a lost object? Describe how the object was found.

3. In your experience, what is one of the biggest obstacles to joy? Explain.

4. Read Luke 15. To which story do you most relate: the lost sheep, the lost coin, or the lost son? Why?

5. Have you ever been lost? Who found you? What did you learn from that experience?

6. To which brother in the Parable of the Lost Son do you most relate? Split the group in half and have one half make a defense for the father's decision to throw a party and the other half make a defense for the older brother's refusal to join the party.

7. Do you know a "lost son"? Write that person's name and pray for that person now.

This week I will set up a meal with _____ to focus on building a relationship through which I can introduce my friend to Jesus. During our meal, I will concentrate on being like the father in the Parable of the Lost Son.

CHAPTER 13: VISION

For Personal Study and Reflection: Look into a mirror. List the first five things you notice about yourself.

Look at a picture of one of your closest friends. List the first five things you notice about your friend.

Reflect on what you noticed in the mirror and the picture. What things did you see that were similar? What things did you see that were different?

For Group Study and Discussion: Ask group members to list the top ten things they notice about other people in the room—what they're wearing, the color of their hair or eyes, where they're sitting, etc. Take some time and compare lists. Did anyone notice the same things? Did anyone notice a detail that doesn't really exist? Who noticed the most unique thing?

1. What keeps us from seeing ourselves for who we really are? What keeps us from seeing others for who they really are?

2. Describe a time when your eyes tricked you. Why were you tricked?

3. How many people do you estimate you see on any given day? How many of those people do you know? How many of those people are important to you for one reason or another? Why?

4. Read Luke 19:1-10. Zacchaeus worked really hard to see Jesus. Who's the most famous person you've ever seen? Was it difficult to see that person? If so, what did you have to do to see that person? Would you do it again?

5. If Jesus appeared right now and said, "I must stay at your house today," what would be your first thought? Why?

6. After meeting Jesus, Zacchaeus promised to give half of his possessions to the poor and to pay back four times the amount he had cheated people. What does this tell you about Zacchaeus?

7. As you reflect on your own conversion experience, what changes did you make in your life in response to meeting Jesus?

8. Jesus' purpose on earth was to "seek and to save the lost" (verse 10). What is one thing you can do this week to fulfill a purpose like his?

This week I will set up a meal with _____ to establish or continue building a relationship through which I can introduce my friend to Jesus. During our meal, I will focus on seeing my friend for who he or she can be in Jesus.

About the Author

For more information on eating with sinners, including a church-wide outreach program based on this book, go to www.eatswithsinners.com.

Arron loves to hear from readers! E-mail him at arron@journeychristian.org.

For more information about Arron's speaking and writing ministry, visit the following:

- www.arronchambers.com
- www.journeychristian.org

OTHER BOOKS BY ARRON CHAMBERS

- *Running on Empty: Life Lessons to Refuel Your Faith*
- *Scripture to Live By: True Stories Inspired by the Word of God*
- *Remember Who You Are: Unleashing the Power of an Identity-Driven Life*
- *Go! From Studio Audience to Center Stage*
- *Narrow-Minded Evangelism: Rethinking Evangelism and the Golden Rule from the Less-Traveled Road*
- *Devoted: Isn't It Time to Fall More in Love with Jesus?* (www.devoteddiscipleship.com)

Notes

A WORD BEFORE
1. You can find more information on The Party program at http://www.eats withsinners.com/study/index.php.
2. The sixteen-week Eats with Sinners church-wide study with sermons, lessons, small-group studies, and other resources can be downloaded at http://www.eatswithsinners.com.

INTRODUCTION
1. "Lost and Found Is Busy at Disneyland," UPI, April 10, 2007, http://www .upi.com/Odd_News/2007/04/10/Lost-and-found-is-busy-at-Disneyland /17311176242709/ (accessed December 12, 2016).
2. Michael Wilson, "3 Hungry Days for Deliveryman Stuck in Elevator," *New York Times*, April 6, 2005, http://www.nytimes.com/2005/04/06 /nyregion/3-hungry-days-for-deliveryman-stuck-in-elevator.html?_r=0 (accessed December 12, 2016).
3. More information about the playground we built with the City of Greeley can be found at http://greeleygov.com/activities/parks/avens-village.
4. Gary L. McIntosh, *Growing God's Church: How People Are Actually Coming to Faith Today* (Grand Rapids, MI: Baker, 2016), 93-95.

CHAPTER 1: INTEGRITY
1. Monk Preston, 2002, "The Monk Who Ended the Coliseum Games," The Prayer Foundation, http://www.prayerfoundation.org/favoritemonks/favorite _monks_telemachus_coliseum.htm (accessed December 21, 2016).

CHAPTER 2: ACCESSIBILITY
1. Rick Warren, *The Purpose Driven Church: Every Church Is Big in God's Eyes* (Grand Rapids, MI: Zondervan, 1995), 46.

CHAPTER 3: GRACE

1. Philip Yancey, *What's So Amazing about Grace?* (Grand Rapids: Zondervan, 1997), 11.
2. "Miniature Earth. 2010 edition. Official version," YouTube video, 3:15, posted by Al Lucca, July 21, 2010, https://www.youtube.com/watch?v=i4639vev1Rw.
3. Bernadette D. Proctor, Jessica L. Semega, and Melissa A. Kollar, "Income and Poverty in the United States: 2015," United States Census Bureau, September 13, 2016, https://www.census.gov/library/publications/2016/demo/p60-256.html (accessed December 21, 2016).
4. Danielle Kaeble, Lauren E. Glaze, Anastasios Tsoutis, and Todd D. Minton, "Correctional Populations in the United States, 2014," Bureau of Justice Statistics, December 29, 2015, http://www.bjs.gov/index.cfm?ty=pbdetail&iid=5519 (accessed December 5, 2016).
5. Associated Press, "Blind Man Who Was Beaten by the Police Files a Claim," *New York Times*, May 25, 1989, http://www.nytimes.com/1989/05/25/us/blind-man-who-was-beaten-by-the-police-files-a-claim.html (accessed December 21, 2016).
6. Bono, "Opening Eyes: Bono Awakens the Church to Social Activism," interview by Andy Argyrakis, *Relevant*, March/April 2004, 45.

CHAPTER 4: FAITH

1. Anand Bodh, "Man Faints During Stampede, Ends Up in Morgue," *Times of India*, August 6, 2008, http://timesofindia.indiatimes.com/india/Man_faints_during_stampede_ends_up_in_morgue/articleshow/3331239.cms (accessed March 18, 2016).
2. I'm actually doing this right now. I'm the executive producer and a screenwriter for an upcoming feature film on the life of Gary Hamilton.
3. "North Carolina Man Makes Record Catch with Barbie Fishing Rod," *FoxNews*, August 21, 2008, http://www.foxnews.com/story/2008/08/21/north-carolina-man-makes-record-catch-with-barbie-fishing-rod.html (accessed December 21, 2016).

CHAPTER 5: INTIMACY

1. Brennan Manning, *The Ragamuffin Gospel: Good News for the Bedraggled, Beat-Up, and Burnt Out* (Colorado Springs: Multnomah, 2005), 59.
2. Santos Yao, "The Table Fellowship of Jesus with the Marginalized: A Radical Inclusiveness," *Journal of Asian Mission* 3:1 (2001): 26.
3. Jerome H. Neyrey, "Reader's Guide to Meals, Food and Table Fellowship in the New Testament," University of Notre Dame, https://www3.nd.edu/~jneyrey1/meals.html (accessed December 12, 2016).
4. Yao, "The Table Fellowship of Jesus," 27.

5. Craig Blomberg, *Contagious Holiness: Jesus' Meals with Sinners* (Downers Grove, IL: InterVarsity, 2005), 93.
6. Manning, *Ragamuffin Gospel*, 22.
7. *Merriam-Webster Online Dictionary*, s.v. "extirpate."

CHAPTER 6: TOLERANCE
1. Rick Riley, "Life of Riley," ESPN, May 12, 2014, http://sports.espn.go.com /espnmag/story?section=magazine&id=3789373 (accessed December 22, 2016).
2. Ibid.
3. Ibid.
4. Dan Barry, "He Befriended a Serial Killer, and Opened the Door to God," *New York Times*, March 11, 2007, http://www.nytimes.com/2007/03/11 /us/11land.html (accessed March 18, 2016).
5. Greg Taylor, "Jeffrey Dahmer's Story of Faith," *Christianity Today*, September 1, 2006, http://www.christianitytoday.com/ct/2006/september/34.125.html (accessed December 22, 2016).

CHAPTER 7: RESOLVE
1. Don Meyer, "So, Near and Yet So Far," *Huffington Post*, August 7, 2013, http://www.huffingtonpost.com/don-meyer-phd/so-near-and-yet-so-far_b _3714989.html (accessed March 18, 2017).
2. Adrian Ballantyne, "Moment #15: Giving Up Not an Option," news.com .au, July 11, 2012, http://www.news.com.au/sport/moment-15-giving-up -not-an-option-for-john-stephen-akhwari/news-story/60947bd56b387d7 eec8d917db9f611b3 (accessed December 21, 2016).

CHAPTER 8: URGENCY
1. Matthew L. Wald, "Plane Crew Is Credited for Nimble Reaction," *New York Times*, January 15, 2009, http://www.nytimes.com/2009/01/16 /nyregion/16pilot.html?src=tp (accessed December 22, 2016); and Al Baker, "Flight 1549: From New York to Norad, Testing a Response Network," *New York Times*, February 8, 2009, www.nytimes.com/2009/02/08/nyregion /08plane.html (accessed December 22, 2016).
2. Wald, "Plane Crew Is Credited for Nimble Reaction," *New York Times*.
3. Baker, "Flight 1549: From New York to Norad, Testing a Response Network," *New York Times*.
4. Ibid.
5. Nick Bilton, "Parenting in the Age of Online Pornography," *New York Times*, January 7, 2015, http://www.nytimes.com/2015/01/08/style/parenting-in -the-age-of-online-porn.html (accessed December 12, 2016).

6. "American Teens' Sexual and Reproductive Health," Guttmacher Institute, May 2014, https://www.guttmacher.org/sites/default/files/pdfs/pubs/FB-ATSRH.pdf (accessed December 12, 2016).

7. "Child Maltreatment 2014," U.S. Department of Health & Human Services, Administration for Children and Families, Administration on Children, Youth and Families, Children's Bureau (2016): 51, https://www.acf.hhs.gov/sites/default/files/cb/cm2014.pdf#page=5 (accessed December 22, 2016).

8. "World Birth and Death Rates," Ecology, 2011, http://www.ecology.com/birth-death-rates/ (accessed December 12, 2016).

9. Robert Moffat, quoted in Randy Alcorn, *90 Days of God's Goodness: Daily Reflections That Shine Light on Personal Darkness* (Portland, OR: Multnomah, 2011), 297.

10. Russell Goldman, "US Airways Hero Pilot Searched Plane Twice Before Leaving," *ABC News*, January 15, 2017, http://abcnews.go.com/US/story?id=6658493 (accessed December 22, 2016).

CHAPTER 9: MERCY

1. "Crazy Pastor in Texas Tells Children in Mall that Santa Is Not Real," YouTube video, 3:09, posted by "Shinigama," December 10, 2016, https://www.youtube.com/watch?v=u1xqD9-9RA0 (accessed on December 12, 2016).

CHAPTER 10: HUMILITY

1. William Beebe, as quoted in *Manitoba School Journal*, Vol. XII, no. 3 (November 1950): 11.

2. Arron Chambers, *Running on Empty: Life Lessons to Refuel Your Faith* (Colorado Springs: David C Cook, 2005), 75.

3. When I was little, I thought dropsy was a condition that made it impossible to hold on to glasses of water, Frisbees, footballs, and infants. I was wrong. Dropsy—also called edema—is swelling from excessive accumulation of watery fluid in cells, tissues, or serous cavities.

4. R. C. Foster, *Studies in the Life of Christ: Introduction, the Early Period, the Middle Period, the Final Week* (Grand Rapids, MI: Baker, 1985), 923.

5. J. Michael Kennedy, "Jessica Makes It to Safety—After 58 1/2 Hours," *Los Angeles Times*, October 17, 1987, http://articles.latimes.com/1987-10-17/news/mn-3702_1_jessica-mcclure (accessed December 21, 2016).

6. "Everett Bride Calls off Wedding, Throws Party for the Homeless," *Seattle Times*, June 29, 2005, http://www.seattletimes.com/seattle-news/everett-bride-calls-off-wedding-throws-party-for-the-homeless/ (accessed December 22, 2016).

CHAPTER 11: INVESTMENT

1. Evan Lambert, "Still No Completion Date for 'I-4 Eyesore,'" News 6, November 6, 2013, http://www.clickorlando.com/news/still-no-completion -date-for-i-4-eyesore (accessed December 22, 2016).
2. Søren Kierkegaard, quoted in Joakim Garff, *Søren Kierkegaard: A Biography* (Trenton, NJ: Princeton University Press, 2013), 773.
3. Dietrich Bonhoeffer, *The Cost of Discipleship* (New York: Touchstone, 1995), 89.

CHAPTER 12: JOY

1. Tom Clegg and Warren Bird, *Lost in America: How You and Your Church Can Impact the World Next Door* (Loveland, CO: Group Publishing, 2001), 16.
2. Gabriel Snyder, "Inside Move: Fanatics Laying It on the Line," *Variety*, April 5, 2005, http://www.variety.com/article/VR1117920656.html?category id=1236 &cs=1&s=h&p=0 (accessed December 22, 2016).
3. Penny Lea, "Sing a Little Louder," Holocaust Memorial Day, http://www .internationalwallofprayer.org/A-010-Holocaust-Memorial-Day-Stover.html (accessed December 22, 2016).
4. George Barna, *Re-Churching the Unchurched* (Ventura, CA: Issachar Resources, 2000), 12.

CHAPTER 13: VISION

1. "Victim at Lifeguards' Party," *New York Times*, August 2, 1985, http://www .nytimes.com/1985/08/02/us/victim-at-lifeguards-party.html (accessed December 22, 2016).
2. Wayne Rice, comp. *More Hot Illustrations for Youth Talks: 100 More Attention-Getting Stories, Parables, and Anecdotes* (Grand Rapids, MI: Zondervan, 1996), 120.
3. Foster, *Studies in the Life of Christ*, 1054.
4. Coco Masters, "Postcard: Tojinbo Cliffs," *Time*, June 22, 2009, http:// content.time.com/time/magazine/article/0,9171,1904132,00.html (accessed December 22, 2016).
5. Ibid.
6. Ibid.

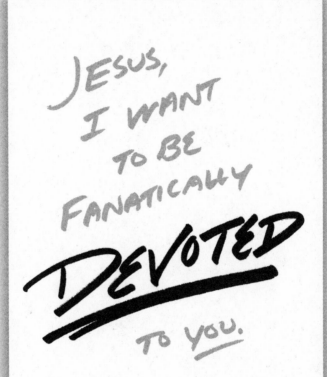

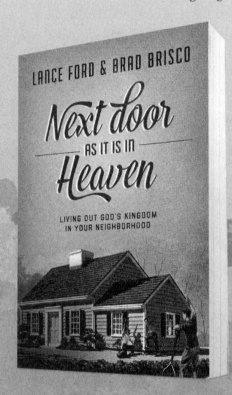

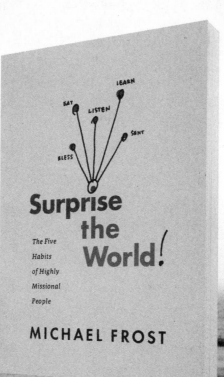